Kelley Library - Salem NH

3 4520 00305585   S0-BRS-033

KELLEY LIBRARY
234 Main Street
Salem, NH 03079
603-898-7064

LP FAITH SPIRITUAL LIVING
Macomber, Debbie.
God's guest list [text (large print)] :
welcoming those who influence our lives
34520003055859

KELLEY LIBRARY
234 Main Street
Salem, NH 03079
603-898-7064

GOD'S GUEST LIST

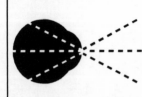

This Large Print Book carries the
Seal of Approval of N.A.V.H.

GOD'S GUEST LIST

WELCOMING THOSE
WHO INFLUENCE OUR LIVES

DEBBIE MACOMBER

THORNDIKE PRESS

A part of Gale, Cengage Learning

Detroit • New York • San Francisco • New Haven, Conn • Waterville, Maine • London

Copyright © 2010 by Debbie Macomber.
Scripture quotations not otherwise marked are taken from the Holy Bible, New International Version ®. Copyright © 1973, 1978, 1984 by International Bible Society. Used by permission of Zondervan. All rights reserved. Scripture quotations marked KJV are taken from the King James Version. Scripture quotations marked NLT are taken from the Holy Bible, New Living, Translation, copyright © 1996, 2004. Used by permission Tyndale House Publishers, Inc., Wheaton, Illinois 60189. All rights reserved. Scripture quotations marked The Message are from The Message. Copyright © 1993, 1994, 1995, 1996, 2000, 2001, 2002. Used by permission of NavPress Publishing Group. All rights reserved.
Thorndike Press, a part of Gale, Cengage Learning.

ALL RIGHTS RESERVED
This work reflects the author's present recollections of her experiences over a period of years. Certain names and identifying characteristics have been changed.
Thorndike Press® Large Print Inspirational.
The text of this Large Print edition is unabridged.
Other aspects of the book may vary from the original edition.
Set in 16 pt. Plantin.

LIBRARY OF CONGRESS CATALOGING-IN-PUBLICATION DATA

Macomber, Debbie.
 God's guest list : welcoming those who influence our lives / by Debbie Macomber. — Large print ed.
  p. cm. — (Thorndike Press large print inspirational)
  Originally published: Nashville, Tenn : Howard Books, c2010.
  Includes bibliographical references (p.).
  ISBN-13: 978-1-4104-3144-8 (hardcover)
  ISBN-10: 1-4104-3144-4 (hardcover)
  1. Influence (Psychology)—Religious aspects—Christianity.
2. Macomber, Debbie. 3. Large type books. I. Title.
BV4597.53.I52M33 2011
248.4—dc22   2010043743

Published in 2011 by arrangement with Howard Books, a division of Simon & Schuster, Inc.

Printed in the United States of America
1 2 3 4 5 6 7 15 14 13 12 11

*To my family,
my husband, Wayne,
and children,
Jody, Jenny, Ted, and Dale.
How very blessed I am
to have you
in my life.*

CONTENTS

ACKNOWLEDGMENTS

Because I write fiction and my God-given talent is that of a storyteller, I never expected to write nonfiction. To be fair, I've contemplated penning a book about writing a time or two but quickly dismissed the idea. The marketplace was flooded with instruction manuals on the topic, and I couldn't see adding to that flood.

Then in 2006 I was approached by my dear friend Wendy Lawton, who suggested I had something other than my writing experiences to share with readers. Wendy is a powerfully persuasive individual, and before I knew it, my first nonfiction title was published. Thus began my foray into the genre of nonfiction. To my utter surprise and delight, I discovered I enjoyed sharing my thoughts and ideas with others.

My prayer is that you'll enjoy reading *God's Guest List* and that it will help you recognize the ones He has sent into your life. I hope you will look at these individuals with fresh eyes and realize how each has shaped you into who you are today.

As always, no book is the product of the author alone. This project idea came from a speech I gave years ago. Wendy Lawton saw it as far more than a simple talk and believed in its potential. As both my dear friend and my agent, she insisted I "dig deep." I dug, Wendy, I dug. Thank you for your vision, your confidence, and your faith in me. Cindy Lambert is an extraordinary editor who took my words and polished them to a bright sheen. You're wonderful. Jonathon Merkh, publisher at Howard Books, is amazing, along with his entire team. I feel blessed to have all of you in my life, guiding me. I know each one of you is part of God's guest list for me.

Lastly, I am so very grateful for the opportunity to share my guest list with you, my readers. May this book inspire, encourage, and challenge you.

Debbie Macomber

Therefore I am sending you
prophets and wise men and teachers.
— MATTHEW 23:34

ONE:
PRESENTS, PEOPLE,
AND ONE MORE LIST

AN UNFINISHED GUEST LIST

There's a story that goes something like this:

A woman arrived at the gates of heaven to be met by St. Peter.

"You may first want to join the others at the throne," he said to her, "and then greet those you loved on earth. But when you are ready, I'll take you on a tour of heaven."

When the time came for her tour, she could hardly take it all in. It reminded her a little of her earthly home, but she could see that earth had only been a pale shadow of what she was seeing now. They explored every nook and cranny of heaven — waterfalls, fields of flowers, exquisite buildings, and streets of gold.

As the tour drew to an end, she noticed one massive door they had not yet explored. A gold padlock secured it. "What's in that room?" she asked.

"You don't want to see that room," St. Peter said, steering her away from it. "It's only a storeroom."

"But I do. May I see inside? I want to see every bit of heaven."

St. Peter didn't answer. Instead he took a large key out of his pocket, put it in the lock, and turned it. The tumblers clicked and the padlock opened. He took the lock off and opened the door. The woman had to blink several times to take it all in. Inside the cavernous room were stacks and stacks of gifts, wrapped in all the colors of the rainbow and tied with all the colors of heaven.

She clapped her hands with delight. "Is this where you store presents for everyone in heaven?"

"No. These gifts are not for heaven, they were meant for earth."

"What do you mean 'were'?" She walked through the stacks and came to a pile marked with her name. "Look, these gifts are for me." She fingered the paper and ribbons. "May I open them?"

"No. You don't need them now." St. Peter put a hand on her shoulder, guiding her toward the door.

"But if I don't need them *now*, does that mean I needed them on earth?" She couldn't take her eyes off the pile. To think she would never get to enjoy all those beautifully wrapped gifts.

He nodded his head. "Yes, you needed them on earth."

She looked around the room, realizing that there must have been millions of gifts. Maybe more, since she couldn't see an end to the room. "Why weren't my gifts sent to me on earth?" As she looked closer, she could read names on all the gifts. "Not just my gifts; why haven't any of these gifts been sent?"

St. Peter sighed. "You don't understand. Every one of them was sent." Moving his arm in an arc that encompassed the whole room, he said, "All of these and more. These are the ones that were returned unopened." He moved her toward the door. "Many people on earth don't recognize God's gifts and fail to open them."

I love gifts — both giving and receiving. When I first heard this story, I wondered if there was any truth to the parable. Had God sent gifts to me that I hadn't opened? When I get to heaven, I don't want to discover that I failed to recognize the gifts God sent into my life. I don't want to miss a single one.

Unfortunately, in real life God's presents don't always come gaily gift-wrapped, and they are not always easily recognized. Some even initially come looking like challenges. And often these gifts are people shaped.

The Second List

If you've read any of my nonfiction books, you know I'm a list maker. Goals, objectives, tasks. They all go on lists. Socrates said, "The unexamined life is not worth living." I've taken his advice to heart and take a careful look at my life day by day in order to make the most of my time and efforts.

Many years ago I read *The Aladdin Factor* by Jack Canfield, who coauthored the Chicken Soup series. This was before that series was as well known as it is now. The one thing I remember most about that book was something Jack Canfield wrote. He made a list of thirty people he wanted to meet in his life. Entertainers, authors, musicians — people whose work he deeply admired and whom he wanted to thank.

What an idea!

It inspired me, and I set about making a list of my own — thirty people I wanted to meet. I started out with Pat Conroy — one of the most gifted writers of our time. The list was filled with people I'd admired throughout my life — writers, musicians, speakers, and others. At the time, the possibility of meeting those on my list seemed impossible, but one by one God brought them into my life, and I gratefully checked them off my list, one by one.

A few years ago I attended a writers' conference. An author from my list whom I'd long admired was to be the keynote speaker. I wanted to tell him the story of how I came to find him and how his writing had inspired me, so it was arranged for us to meet and talk. We sat in a quiet corner of the hotel lobby and I began to tell him what his work has meant to me. Halfway through the story, he stopped me. "Just a minute. You have to stop, because I need to bask." That's B-A-S-K — bask. I didn't know what he meant until he closed his eyes and began to breathe deeply through his nose. He waved his hands as if to fan my words toward him and got a weird look on his face as he appeared to soak in my words of encouragement.

It was all I could do to keep from bursting out laughing. That someone would need to bask in the glory of a simple compliment flabbergasted me. Long after that conference was over, I continued to think about that incident. It was so odd. The more I thought about it, the more disappointed I became in this person. I had held him in such high regard. How could I have been so wrong? Instead of reflecting any glory back to God, this author chose to absorb it for himself. To bask in my praise.

The sad thing is that he wasn't the only one from my list who turned out to be a disappointment. I had listed a well-known, much-loved singer with a career history that spans forty years. The lyrics he sings are so beautiful and touch me deeply, but I came to find out they're lyrics written by other people. It soon became obvious that he was so plastic, so saccharine, that if I had met him in any other circumstance, I confess I would have automatically avoided him. His world revolved around him. Because people had kowtowed to him for so long, he had no patience. His frustration threshold was dangerously low. I watched as he snapped his fingers at people, signaling them to bring him things. It was cringe-worthy. Even more telling, his annoyance and rudeness turned to smiles the moment someone lifted a camera in his direction. Sad.

During my morning prayer time, shortly after my visit with the author at the writers' conference, I found myself telling God how disillusioned I was with so many of the people on my list. It didn't take too many disappointments to conclude that unless the person stayed God-centered, fame and talent seemed to ruin the person in some way. Basking in their own accomplishments led to self-absorption and self-obsession. Many of them didn't even seem to see other people. So that morning I complained to God how disappointed I was in several of the people on my list. Then it hit me. My disappointment stemmed not from the fact that these people were flawed. We are all flawed. The true source of my disappointment was that I had misplaced my admiration.

As I prayed, I sensed that God was saying, *There is a reason I had that happen, Debbie. It's because I want you to make another list. You asked Me to send those thirty people into your life. You're My daughter. I love you, and as your Father, I want to give you the things that you ask for, but I also wanted you to see people through My eyes. Now make another list and put down thirty more spaces, but leave them open for the people I want to send into your life.*

God would send people into my life? An open list. A guest list. It was as if He had issued invitations to my life and asked me to watch for the people He would be sending.

What a concept!

Knowing that God had already compiled a guest list filled me with anticipation — a

21

sense of discovery. From that point on I've looked deeply into each face I meet. Could this be one of the guests God invited into my life? Little by little, I've been filling in those spaces on that list. And you know what? I have yet to be disappointed with God's guest list for my life.

This list has become one of the most important lists in my life. I call it God's guest list. Though I arbitrarily started with thirty blanks, a finite number unnecessarily limits this list. God's guest list for my life is meant to be lived out as an open invitation, welcoming those whom God sends our way.

I know that God is sovereign. He sends every person we meet into our lives, but I'm talking about a list of special guests — the ones who have changed us, or who will change us, in some significant way. They don't necessarily have to be our closest friends. Sometimes you'll read something by someone that affects you deeply. You may never even meet that person, but you discover that God sent him or her into your life.

One of my friends has been deeply affected by the writings of C. S. Lewis. He died when she was only a child, but the things she learned from Lewis have forever changed her. If she were making her list,

Lewis would certainly be on it even though she will never meet him this side of heaven.

Recognizing those who will influence us is no easy task. Sometimes we meet someone and are immediately drawn to that person, confident that he or she may very well be an important part of our life. We might even seek someone out. And at times we may even feel like our life has been invaded by someone we'd rather have avoided, only to discover that God sent that person, wrote that person on our list, for His own surprising purposes.

Living with Our Eyes Wide Open

Filling out our lists will take a lifetime. It's not something that can be ticked off a task list in an afternoon. But if we commit to discovering God's guest list for our lives, we will move through life with our eyes wide open. Here's a promise from the Lord: "Therefore I am sending you prophets and wise men and teachers" (Matthew 23:34). It's up to us to recognize them. When we start searching, we'll begin to look deeply into every person we meet to see if we can find God's fingerprints on that person. We don't want to send a single gift back unopened.

I've begun to practice this with people I

meet as well. Whether at the grocery store, in my family, among friends, at church, in my industry, or in the line at a book signing, when I'm on the lookout for those who may be on God's guest list, I've come to appreciate people in a whole new way. Even those who are just passing through become reminders of God's gifts to me. That sense of anticipation and awareness heightens the fun of meeting people.

As writer Ashleigh Brilliant quips, "My life has a superb cast, but I can't figure out the plot."[1]

In the pages of this book, I'll share what I've discovered from my own guest list. As I tell you stories about these people, you'll see how they've changed me. And hopefully you'll see God's hand in my life. Be assured, however, this book isn't about me. I want to tell you these stories so you can see how God works and begin to look for His fingerprints on your own life. It's a quest that could very well change your outlook and your attitude toward others the way it changed my own.

Each guest that God brings into our lives leaves us with a unique gift. Once I fully understood this truth, I began to intentionally look for and recognize these gifts. To help you compile your own Gift List, look for this *Gifts from Our Guests* feature throughout the book.

> *Gifts from Our Guests:* The gift of seeing God at work through life's guests gives us new eyes to see and appreciate God like never before.

The List

Why do we create a physical list? Isn't it enough to simply look at all people as the potential VIPs of our lives?

It is important because the list itself is part of the discipline. Remember Socrates' unexamined life? He said such a life is not worth living. If we want to live a fulfilling life, we need to examine it. The key to accomplishing any discipline in life, whether it is setting goals, losing weight, changing behavior, or discovering God's guest list, is to be intentional, to be aware, and to be able to chart our findings. Discovering God's guest list is the same. We write it down because it becomes a chronicle of our journey.

You could keep God's guest list in your daily journal, your prayer journal, or your gratitude journal if you use those. You may want to buy a special journal to log your discoveries and annotate the names you

25

add. Or you could keep your list right here.
I've given you thirty slots but I hope you fill
up all the slots and run out of room for all
the people God sends.

1. _____

2. _____

3. _____

4. _____

5. _____

6. _____

7. _____

8. _____

9. _____

10. _____

11. _____

12. _____

13. _____

14. _____

15. _____

16. _____

17. _____

18. _____

19. _____

20. _____

21. _____

22. _____

23. _____

24. _____

25. _____

26. _____

27. _____

28. _____

29. _____

30. _____

RSVP

The letters RSVP stand for the French expression *répondez s'il vous plaît,* meaning "please respond." The purpose of this book is to help us identify and welcome those special people God sends into our lives, but if we believe that God has a hand-picked guest list for our lives, it stands to reason that He'll have us on the guest lists for others' lives. Throughout the book, when you see the words RSVP, we'll be turning the tables and examining our own potential influence in the lives of others.

I'm challenging you, as you begin to discover the guest list for your own life, to also be intentional about your influence in the lives around you.

*Wisdom is enshrined
in an understanding heart.*
— PROVERBS 14:33 (NLT)

Two:
An Olympian, a Homeless Man, and Lost Luggage
WISE MEN AND WOMEN

I read a book this year that changed my life. It's called *Breakfast at Sally's: One Homeless Man's Inspirational Journey.* How often does a book change our whole way of looking at a situation? This one did for me. The author, Richard LeMieux, was once a successful businessman who owned cars and boats and a luxury home. When his business failed, he began to lose every vestige of his successful life — his wife, his family, and even his home. When we meet him in the pages of his memoir, he's homeless and living in a beat-up Oldsmobile van with his dog, Willow. Penniless and hungry, he depends on the kindness of strangers for each meal.

Throughout the book, LeMieux shares the wisdom and kindness of the men he meets on the street in Bremerton, Washington. After LeMieux put flesh and blood, hopes and dreams, on the nameless, homeless street people, I will never look at them in the same way again. I know that God put Richard LeMieux and his unforgettable memoir on my list.

Gifts from Our Guests: Guests bringing the gift of wisdom come in an assortment of packages — from the scholar and sage to the homeless man or woman.

The Four-Minute Mile

My friend Rhett Palmer interviews celebrities from every walk of life. The one question he traditionally asks is "Who was the biggest influence in your life?" I loved the answer Jim Ryun — the first high-school athlete to run the four-minute mile — gave Rhett.

God gave me my talent but I attribute my success to my coach, who had a wonderful vision. At the end of my fourth high school race we were riding the school bus back from Kansas City to Wichita. It was about a three-hour ride. Coach always saved a seat up in the front of the bus for each of the athletes to come up, sit down, and talk with him, at which point he would reflect on their race for that day and give them a challenge.

He sat me down and said, "Jim you ran a great race. How fast do you think you can run?"

That day I had run a 4:21 mile; I was slowly improving.

He said, "I think that you could be the school record holder."

I knew that the school record holder was also the national record holder — at that time a guy named Archie Sanbumonti with a 4:08 mile. In the sport of running, going from 4:21 to 4:08 was phenomenal.

He said, "I think that you can be the first high school boy to run the mile in under four minutes." So he began planting that particular vision in my life, which I think ultimately led to my making the Olympic team — running under four minutes in high school in 1963.

If you go back to 1954, Dr. Roger Bannister was the first man to run it in under four minutes. Now we are talking about a skinny kid who was cut from his church baseball team and couldn't make the junior high basketball team — making his first Olympic team as a seventeen-year-old.

So I attribute that success to my wonderful coach and the great talent God gave me.

Gifts from Our Guests: God sometimes calls the very people who can bring the gift of a vision for our future to join our guest list. If we recognize them, our lives will never be the same.

The Eye of an Editor

I wonder how many other fiction writers can say they've had the same editor for twenty-four years. When I think of the wise women in my life, Paula Eykelhof comes to mind. We grew up in this industry of writing together. We've always joked about our relationship being like Helen Keller and Anne Sullivan's, only we don't always know who is who — we keep changing places.

When I first began thinking about doing a novel based on knitting — the book that would eventually become *The Shop on Blossom Street* — I pictured a pattern book for a baby blanket that would be passed from character to character. When I told Paula, she wasn't enthusiastic, so I put it on the back burner. The story wouldn't leave me, and I kept revisiting it. About two years later I called Paula and said, "You know that knitting story I've been thinking about?

What about if I set it in a knitting store and everyone knit the same pattern but each one had a different reason for knitting it?"

Paula didn't hesitate. "Yes, Debbie, now it's a book." She could see that rather than unconnected characters, an ensemble cast would make the book come alive.

That's the eye of a good editor.

Lost Luggage

With this book in mind, I recently asked a friend if God had brought some wise men or women into her life. She told me about her friend, Dr. Herbert Opalek. His story is one I will never forget.

Rabbi Herb Opalek looked at the clock on the hotel nightstand: 1:00 A.M. Sleep eluded him. He had flown into Boston earlier in the day, but his luggage never made it. Now he found himself in a lonely hotel room, watching Ted Koppel. All he had with him were the clothes on his back, his black hat, the courtesy airline toiletry bag, his prayer book, and one volume of the Mishna — the Jewish Oral Law.

He picked up the book, but there was little between the covers he didn't already know. He could recite most of it by heart. The rabbi was known in Orthodox circles as one of the great minds of Jewish law. He had taught at universities and rabbinical seminaries. He was currently the executive vice president of one of the largest seminaries in New York.

Opening the drawer of the nightstand, he found a Gideon Bible. He opened it to a chapter in John and began to read. He was already familiar with the book. His Ph.D. studies had centered on varieties of the Jewish religion in the first century A.D. He had studied the Bible — Genesis through Revelation — in the original Hebrew, Aramaic, and Greek. But something was different. Dr. Opalek says, "On that night and in that room, for the very first time in my life, I encountered the Holy Spirit and allowed God to permeate my being."

Dr. Opalek calls it his Damascus road experience. The rabbi encountered the God he thought he had always known. He suddenly knew what God required of him — to accept God's own Son, Jesus. The enormity of it frightened him. "I was scared out of my skull," he said. When he got back to New York City, he did what any Jewish scholar would do. He tested this new understanding to see if it were truth from God or deception from Satan. "I prayed. And I went to the New York City Library and began to study the scriptures in earnest, without bias," Dr. Opalek said. "The truth became apparent."

So what does a respected, well-known rabbi do when he comes face-to-face with Christ? People often say that when they made the decision to follow Christ, their life was never again the same. With Dr. Opalek, that would be an understatement.

Herbert Opalek had been destined to become a rabbi from the time he was born. The only child of doting parents, he had been sanctified to serve God. He grew up in Brooklyn in the same community Chaim Potok describes in *The Chosen.* Dr. Opalek still has an old 16mm roll of film showing him at the age of four acting as rabbi at his cousin's wedding rehearsal.

He distinguished himself in school and studied under many renowned European rebbes. By the time he was ten he could hold a fluent conversation in Hebrew, both ancient and modern. Dr. Opalek has a near photographic memory. He tells of making money and finagling many a free dinner by performing his famous pin trick. "I would take a volume of the Talmud and allow a person to push a pin into it. I knew the book so well, I could judge the page, the line, and the letter on which the point of the pin rested."

Dr. Opalek often says he identifies with Paul: "I was a Pharisee of the Pharisees and a Jew of all Jews." There are three different levels of rabbis. Some Jews are given an honorific title of Rabbi when they marry. Then there are the teachers — *Yoreh Yoreh.* The third level are the judges, *Yodin Yodin.* Opalek was an ecclesiastical judge, a Yodin Yodin. He judged civil law.

When it came time to marry, the wife chosen for Opalek was a direct descendant of David. The marriage would be a stunning partnership — the brilliant scholar to the family of antiquity and spiritual greatness. The rabbi was poised for greatness.

What happened that night in the Boston hotel room changed everything. His decision to follow Christ turned his world upside down.

"Had my parents been alive," Opalek says, "I don't know that I could have dishonored them. But God has a way of doing things in His own time." As it was, Dr. Opalek lost everything, including family and friends. He resigned from his position at the research institute. The community vilified him. As he walked through the city, he would cross the street to avoid being spat upon. Former friends played cruel pranks — like having three hundred pizzas delivered to his door.

So where does a rabbi go when he's no longer part of the community in which he lived and worked? At first he thought he might go into a Catholic monastery, but as he investigated, he knew it wouldn't work. "In all my years as a rabbi, I never needed an intercessor to speak to God. Why would I start now?"

He looked into a Protestant seminary, but he already had the book knowledge. He needed the heart knowledge far more than the head knowledge. Where does one go to grow faith? Ever the scholar, he did an on-line search and found a Lexis article on the New York Rescue Mission. The article stated that their mission was to "bring people to faith." Dr. Opalek had no community, no family and nowhere to live. He showed up at the door of the rescue mission and found a home — both physically and spiritually. He eventually ended up on staff.

"It was the perfect place for me," Dr. Opalek says with grin. "I'm a little on the prideful side — I was always mindful of how far I had gone and how much I had achieved. Coming to the mission humbled me. I was like the psalmist: 'Out of the depths I cried out.' " He could relate to the people they served. "Cleaning up vomit on the floor and assisting guests to delouse in the showers further humbled me." He began to understand the kind of servanthood Christ talks about.

The director of the mission became his spiritual guide. "We fought like cats and dogs," Dr. Opalek remembers, "but he wasn't afraid of my intellect and he wasn't easily intimidated."

Eight months after coming to Christ, Dr. Opalek found himself heading up to the Albany Rescue Mission to take on the position of special assistant to the director. He laughs at the irony of becoming a Christian counselor in the same year he became a Christian.

Dr. Herb Opalek found his spiritual home in the rescue mission ministry and he's been in it ever since, now serving as director of the Merced County Rescue Mission in central California. He's also chairman of the board for Rescue Israel, the first American-style rescue mission in Israel. "Since I was rescued that's what God called me to do — rescue others."

Gifts from Our Guests: Our faith is enriched to hear our guests' stories — to see how God moved into their lives. And when they move into the lives of others, He moves with them.

Against All Odds

I am so thankful for the wise women in my life. Lillian is one of those wise women. She's a member of my breakfast club and has been a source of encouragement to me for years.

When I first started working outside the home, I began having to make decisions for which I felt totally inadequate. Lillian, who rented the office downstairs from my first office, is an attorney, but few attorneys have a story like hers.

After a troubled childhood she married at only fourteen years of age. She had no high school experience. At age seventeen she and her teenage husband already had two children. It sounds like a recipe for catastrophe, but after her own children started off to school, Lillian went back to complete her education. She got her GED, went on to college, then to law school, passed the bar, and became an attorney. What are the chances? Hers is just an amazing story of survival — a testament to what God can do in a life.

And for me, she was a constant source of encouragement. I learned from her, watched her success, and modeled myself after her.

Wise Counsel

One of the talents God gave me is recognizing the talent of others. I would be remiss if I didn't mention two very special people God has brought into my life whose wisdom and examples have added such value to my life and my writing career.

The first is Nancy Berland, my personal publicist. I first got to know Nancy when she was the volunteer publicist for a national writers' conference at which I was the keynote speaker. Nancy had me on every radio and television station in town. She arranged for me to be interviewed by several newspapers as well.

When I commented on what a good job she'd done, Nancy was quick to brush off the praise. Perhaps she was surprised by my praise because, as she explained, although many years earlier she had worked as a publicist, she had given it up when she married.

After the conference I approached Nancy and encouraged her to consider opening her own publicity agency. I told her that if she would agree to do that, I would be her first client and would bring her others. She did, and today Nancy has the largest author-driven publicity agency in the country.

Not only has she been successful in her

endeavor, but she has been both a friend and advisor to me. I don't make a business decision without first consulting Nancy. She's responsible for my website and my annual newsletter, which is mailed out to my reader list, and she is invaluable to me in more ways than I can enumerate. Nancy Berland is wise and gifted and is herself a gift God brought into my life.

Another wise woman whose talent I recognized is our pastor's wife, Marcia Hestead. First, a bit of backstory. My mother kept a meticulous home and yard. She loved working in her yard, and I inherited the same love. Unfortunately I simply don't have the time or inclination to keep up my yard the way I once did. There are simply too many other pulls on my time, and I had to set priorities. For years my husband, Wayne, and I used a lawn service, and while they did a good job of maintaining our yard, it never met my standards. Then I learned that our pastor's wife wanted to get into landscaping. When I approached her about maintaining our lawns and flowerbeds, she agreed. I was her first customer. She took over my yard, designing flowerbeds and refiguring the landscape. Before long I had the yard I'd always dreamed of. As other people saw how beautifully maintained my yard was, demand for her services increased, so Marcia started her own company, Out of the House Landscaping, Inc. When I arrive home from the office, Marcia is often working in my yard, with her iPod playing Christian music. We chat, and I come away blessed in a multitude of ways — graced by her friendship and wisdom.

Gifts from Our Guests: Wise role models enrich our guest lists and often bring the gift of expanding horizons into our lives.

As we go through life with our eyes wide open, we need to take special note of the wise people God has sprinkled across our path. Every time I read the book of Proverbs, I am reminded again that we are to "get wisdom."

If we are going to be intentional about seeking wisdom, we need to know where to seek it. The writer of Proverbs gave some great guidelines:

- **Seek wise people.** "Let the wise listen and add to their learning, and let the discerning get guidance" (1:5).
- **Two (or more) heads are better than one.** "Plans fail for lack of counsel, but with many advisers they succeed" (15:22).
- **Look for good people.** "The heart of the righteous weighs its answers, but the mouth of the wicked gushes evil" (15:28).
- **Don't be afraid of tough love.** "He who rebukes a man will in the end gain more favor than he who has a flattering tongue" (28:23).
- **A little iron never hurt anyone.** "As iron sharpens iron, so one man sharpens another" (27:17).

RSVP

I met yet another person from my original list of thirty as I was writing this book. Thanks to the introduction from a friend, I had lunch with John Maxwell and his wife, Margaret. I'd long wanted to meet John to tell him how much his books on leadership influenced my own leadership style. Because I'd used several of his devotionals for my own quiet times, I already felt like I'd known him for years. John and Margaret were delightful in person. We visited, swapped stories, and discovered we had many things in common.

One of the stories John related underscored how important it can be to RSVP to God's invitation to influence others. The Maxwells had just returned from a trip to China, where John had spoken at a major university in Beijing. He told us how surprised he was when the academic dean stood up to introduce him. The dean picked up a book by Mao Zedong in one hand and one by Lenin in the other. He said, "For many years these were the two books we read on leadership." He put the books down and picked up John Maxwell's book, *The 21 Irrefutable Laws of Leadership.* "This is our guidebook now."

We don't often get to see the effects of our influence like John did that morning. Can you imagine how exciting to find out that your ideas could potentially influence a nation of young leaders? Chances are we will never have that kind of sweeping influence, but I'm pretty sure God wants us to be just as faithful whether it's one little child or an entire continent we're influencing.

Two are better than one,
because they have a good
return for their work:
If one falls down,
his friend can help him up.
But pity the man who falls
and has no one to help him up!
— ECCLESIASTES 4:9–10

THREE:
FRIENDS FOR A SEASON, FRIENDS FOR A REASON, AND THE ONES THAT GOT AWAY

FRIENDS

When I gave birth to my second child, Jenny, I shared a room in the hospital with another mom. What a bonding time — we both had our new babies at the same time. She and her husband were young, just as Wayne and I were — really young. They had lived in the drug world before coming to personal faith in Jesus. They experienced a significant transformation, and he had gone into the ministry. Wayne and I were brand-new Christians. After we checked out of the hospital, we continued our friendship. As we were exploring this new faith as young Christians, they were there to encourage us. What good times we had together! But as often happens in the overwhelming lives of young families, when they moved away, we lost touch with them. We've never reconnected, but I often think of this couple when people talk about friends for a season. God had these people on my guest list for a time when I needed a friend who could help me grow in my fledgling faith.

Friends for a Season

That friend was much like Marilyn Kimmel. I met Marilyn when Wayne and I moved into our new neighborhood. My life was never the same again. As a young wife and mother, she had decided our neighborhood would be her ministry. She walked down the street with a Bible in her hand and silently prayed, claiming each house for God. What a bold claim of faith. How grateful I am that she prayed over my house. It was through Marilyn that I met the Lord, when she invited me to attend Bible Study Fellowship. Wayne and I had already had Jody and Jenny when we moved into that neighborhood, but soon Ted arrived, followed by Dale two years later. It wasn't long until we were bursting at the seams of that little house. We moved away, and although Marilyn and I kept in touch, our busy lives made it difficult.

But even as a friend for a season, Marilyn changed my life by her example, her willingness to share her own love for Jesus, and her invitation to join her in studying God's Word. I can't imagine what I would be like now had she not been faithful to her ministry in the neighborhood where God planted us.

Gifts from Our Guests: Sometimes God sends us guests who will change our lives simply by their living example of a life well lived or priorities well chosen or values well demonstrated. Such a guest need not have a long stay in our lives to have a huge impact.

Friends for a Reason

I've been surprised by the friends God put on my guest list for a specific reason. Linda Rohrbough, a fellow writer, is one of those. I met Linda in Amarillo, Texas, where I went for a conference. While I was there, another writer, Jodi Thomas, whom I had long admired, invited me to lunch at her house. I didn't know it at the time, but Jodi was coming back from a lengthy speaking engagement and had arrived home just the night before. She was exhausted. Her friend Linda said to her, "Let me help you." That's the way Linda is.

Linda lived near Dallas, but she came to Amarillo — no short distance — to help Jodi host the luncheon. She prepared a delicious meal, and while we were eating, Linda sat across from me. She barely ate anything.

At first I didn't notice, because we rarely notice what other people eat. We tend to be focused on our own food.

After the lunch Linda did the dishes so Jodi could visit with her guests. Once the kitchen was all cleaned up, Jodi and Linda offered to show me Amarillo. The three of us rode around town, looking at the historic homes and the antique district. It was a treat for me because I love to catch the flavor of a town but rarely get the time to do any sightseeing. And, of course, the whole time we drove, we talked. Jodi mentioned to me that Linda had lost 136 pounds. Because I have had a lifetime weight problem, that caught my attention. I asked, "What kind of diet were you on?"

She said, "It wasn't a diet at all. I had weight-loss surgery."

That was not something I had ever considered — too risky for me. I said, "I know I need to lose weight, but I'm not interested in drastic surgery." I probably also said something about it being a faith struggle.

She surprised me when she answered, "The surgery isn't drastic, it's completely reversible." She told me about the LAP-BAND surgery, also called adjustable gastric band surgery. I had never heard of it before. She was writing a book about it with her surgeon, so she answered every question I could think to ask. By the time I left Amarillo, I was seriously considering the surgery.

After I was home, she sent me even more information. I was definitely interested but kept arguing with myself. Wasn't my weight a spiritual problem that I had battled over the years? Would God approve of a quick fix instead of the discipline I needed to develop? Despite these misgivings, I went to my doctor and talked to him about it. He referred me to another doctor, one who specialized in bariatrics. At that time, four or five years ago, hardly anybody had heard of the surgery. Only a few procedures were being done.

Linda continued to stay in touch, encouraging me and answering questions. I ended up deciding to have the procedure. It's made a complete difference in my life both physically and spiritually.

As I looked back in my journals, especially my prayer journals, I saw that every single day I dragged my weight problem before the Lord, and every single day I asked for forgiveness for having failed Him in some way or another. My weight had become the focus of my spiritual life, drowning other areas of my life that needed attention.

As I began slowly and safely losing the

weight after surgery, other spiritual issues came to the forefront that had nothing to do with the number on my scale. It became apparent to me that my weight had been a roadblock that Satan had erected, one that I kept butting my head up against until I was spiritually black and blue, battered senseless, and deeply wounded. I had been so convinced that if God loved me, He would have shown me a way to accomplish this on my own. And if I was a good enough Christian, I should have been able to do it, because heaven knows I dieted enough.

That roadblock kept me from getting on with my spiritual growth.

I didn't lose the weight overnight, and I learned that the band is just a tool to help one learn new eating habits and exercise skills. I don't get on the scale very often, because weighing myself isn't important anymore. In the past if I thought I might have lost weight for any reason, I would step on a scale. That scale dominated my life. It would cause me to think, *Gee, how do I feel about myself today? Let me weigh myself and see.*

So even though I've lost nearly ninety pounds, the change in me is so much more than physical or even emotional. The spiritual changes in me have been the real surprise. That roadblock has been flattened, and I can see the path that God had laid out for me. He'd been waiting there on the other side all along.

I just had to come to a point where I was willing to surrender and say, "I can't do this." My prayer had always been that I would be strong enough, that I could accomplish this. That's where I went wrong — I couldn't do it on my own. If anyone could have done it, it would have been me. In every other area of my life I'm such a goal-oriented person. I am disciplined, and I know what's important to me. My relationship with God, my career, my family, and my passions are what are most important. I thank God for His sending Linda into my life.

This reminds me of the story of the woman who sat on the roof of her house, floodwaters creeping up to the eaves. She prayed that God would rescue her. Not long afterward, a boat came rowing by, and the person offered her a ride to dry land. "No, thank you," she said. "God is going to rescue me."

As she continued to ask that God rescue her, sirens interrupted her prayer. A fire truck had parked on the rise by her house and was lowering an extension ladder in her direction. She waved them off. She knew God would rescue her. As the water continued to rise, a helicopter flew overhead and lowered a bucket with a rescue worker toward her. She refused to go, preferring to wait on the Lord.

While still praying, the woman perished in the floodwaters. As she entered heaven, the first thing she asked the Lord was, "Why didn't you save me? I kept praying."

The Lord just smiled at her as He would at a little child. "I sent a boat. I sent a fire truck. I sent a helicopter. But each time you waved it away."

I was like that woman on the rooftop until my friend Linda came along and rescued me. She's a great example that God sometimes puts friends in our lives for a reason.

Gifts from Our Guests: The best of friends know how to give us the special gift of recognizing our blind spots.

Friends Who Believe

We met Norm and Sharon Frelinger many years ago when Wayne and Norm were first apprentice electricians together. In fact, we knew Norm before he even met Sharon. At first I found Sharon hard to get to know, but as our friendship deepened, she became the best kind of friend — one who believes in me without reservation.

Before my first book was published, Sharon used to listen to me tell her stories as we walked together. She loved my stories and pressed me to tell more. She always said, "Debbie, you are going to be published. Don't ask me how I know. I just know."

That is what a struggling writer needs to hear.

When I got my very first rejection notice, Sharon sent flowers with a note that said, "You are going to be far more successful than you can ever dream!"

That is what a struggling writer needs to hear.

And to this day she continues to believe in me. I've had a successful 2009 Hallmark Channel movie, *Mrs. Miracle,* and we're planning another for next year, but one of my dreams is to see a book become a major motion picture.

Guess what Sharon says: "It's going to happen, Debbie."

Gifts from Our Guests: The nicest gift a friend can give us is encouragement —

59

that, and a belief that our dreams will come true.

The Ones That Got Away

When I reflect on how God moves through our interactions with others, I realize that sometimes I have been able to see the need for allowing people into my life even more clearly through those I didn't let in. I remember in particular one woman I'd met through a Bible study we both attended. She had several children, and they often asked to come to my house. I had my four little ones — stair-stepped in age — and when you added her kids to the mix it wore me out. She never reciprocated and she seemed perfectly happy to let me have her children all day, every day. I finally got to the point where I couldn't deal with it any longer. I wanted to break off the friendship because it was such a needy family, and I had my own children's needs to see to.

It wasn't until later that we found out the father was sexually abusing her girls. I continue to think back with regret. If only I'd been able to read the signs. If only I could've seen it, recognized it, and helped them. The father went to prison and the couple divorced, but I will always be sorry I missed the opportunity to stand in the gap for those little girls and their mother. I regret something more — my resentment of the fact that she didn't have my children over to her home. All the time I was nurturing that resentment, she may have been protecting my children from the danger in her home. What might have happened if I had gone to her in honest communication and opened up to her about my thoughts. Might she have opened up to me?

I wish I could say that I've never missed a chance to reach out and help other friends since then. But life is busy, and I fear I often miss opportunities to do so.

Like the Christmas when I'd planned to go shopping with friends. As I drove down our lane, I saw my elderly neighbor sitting outside, slouched against the trunk of an apple tree. She seemed to have a blank look on her face. It was December. Cold and damp December. I rolled the window down. "Paula, are you all right? Do you need me to call somebody?"

And she said, "No, no, no, no, I'm just very sad."

I should have stopped to talk to her right then, but I was already late, and I'd be holding everyone up and . . . well, you know how it is.

Later, as I returned, I saw the sign on the

reader board outside what had been her son's business. It read, "Happy Birthday, Al." No wonder Paula was sad. It was his birthday — her son who had been murdered earlier that summer. Here was yet another opportunity I missed to minister to someone in need.

> *Gifts from Our Guests:* There are going to be potential friends with whom we never manage to connect. We will miss opportunities to show friendship as well. Those missed opportunities offer the gift of a second chance — maybe not with that person, but with someone else.

Unexpected Friendship

When Wayne and I first moved to Florida, we bought a condominium and renovated it. Because I work so much, I wasn't able to connect with the other people in the complex. When you live in a Florida condo, the social center of the community is the swimming pool. Many of the residents would go down in the afternoons and gather around the pool.

Because I write and have deadlines, I was seldom able to socialize around the pool. If I swam at all, it was early in the morning or late, late in the afternoon. So, I didn't have the chance to meet a lot of the people.

One day there was a notice that one of our neighbors was scheduled to give a lecture on the Civil War. Wayne is fascinated by anything having to do with the Civil War, so we decided we would attend this lecture. It would provide an excellent opportunity to get to know neighbors as well.

What a good decision that was! Gary Roche, the speaker, was not only fascinating, but his great-great-grandfather was a recipient of the Medal of Honor from the Civil War. Gary now has that Medal of Honor in his possession. Wayne was an instant admirer.

Over the years, Gary and Marsha, his wife, have become our good friends. Of all the condo buildings that we could have moved into, we chose the one with someone who has this unique interest in the Civil War — the same interest as Wayne's.

For the last three summers, Gary, who is a licensed battlefield guide, has taken us to Gettysburg and given us detailed tours. When Wayne first wanted to go to Gettysburg for our vacation to do this tour, I hesitated, but I thought that Marsha and I could go to antique stores or yarn stores. I figured I'd just drive around with them and sit in the backseat and knit.

Well, Gary had such wonderful stories about the Civil War and that time period that soon my knitting was stuffed in the bag and I was leaning forward, listening to the stories. Thanks to Gary I have gained a deep appreciation of that time in our history and the changes it brought about in our country.

Gary introduced us to Bob Mullen, who was also known as Mr. Gettysburg. His insight and knowledge of the battle made him a highly sought-after Gettysburg historian. Wayne and I had the privilege of sitting on Bob's back porch discussing the battle with Gary, Marsha, and a number of other battlefield guides. We feel blessed beyond measure to have had this opportunity. Sadly, Bob died early in 2010, and while we miss him, both Wayne and I will be forever grateful for the opportunity we had to call him friend.

God had a dual purpose in putting Gary and Marsha on our guest lists. For Wayne, it was the gift of a friend who shared his fascination with the history of our country. For me it was the gift of a fellow storyteller.

Gifts from Our Guests: Friends can give the gift of opening us up to new experiences. Sometimes we are given the gift of

sharing together something we already
love, and our joy is doubled.

So how do we recognize those potential friends God may have put on our guest lists? I told the stories of opportunities that got away. Everyone is sure to have them. It makes us wonder how different our lives may have been had we recognized those friends.

I think it takes a combination of intentionally seeking people to whom we are drawn and keeping our eyes open for those who are complete surprises. When we intentionally seek people out, it helps to know what we value in a friend. It wouldn't hurt to write down some of the things you appreciate most in a friend. We need to have friends who stretch us and ones we admire. We love to have friends who share our interests and those who teach us new things. Write it down and keep your eyes open. We may not be like the four-year-old who goes up to a child on the playground and says, "Will you be my friend?" but we can find ways to connect to see if friendship grows.

And then there are those surprise friends. These may not be the people who share any of the traits you've listed, and yet they come into our lives and we are never the same. Sometimes these people need us more than we need them, but when we take stock, we realize they've brought far more into our lives than we ever expected.

Part of taking note is just paying attention.

RSVP

With several of the friend stories I shared, I lost track of the friends because of moves or busyness. Now I try to be much more intentional about treasuring the friends on God's guest list for my life.

Here are some things we can all do:

- Make sure to stay in touch with friends. It takes being intentional, but it is too easy with our crazy busy lifestyles to let people drift away.
- Work to keep our address books current. I'd hate to think I lost track because of a move I didn't record until after the forwarding address had expired.
- Connect with each other at least once a year. People groan at the thought of Christmas cards as a way to stay in touch, but I find it to be a good discipline. I especially appreciate getting Christmas letters — despite those who mock them. I want to know about the triumphs and changes in friends' families. It doesn't matter to me that it is not a personal letter. It's an efficient way to keep our many friends connected.
- Keep a record of special contributions.

Some people keep a people journal. I think that's a wonderful idea. I'd love to have a page or two for every friend with a photo and many of the wise things they've said to me. What a treasure it would be.

As François duc de La Rochefoucauld once said, "A true friend is the greatest of all blessings, and that which we take the least care of all to acquire."[1]

Dear friend, you are faithful in what you are doing for the brothers, even though they are strangers to you.
— 3 JOHN 1:5

FOUR:
A SPILLED LATTE, A CONGRESSMAN'S COMPASSION, AND SHRIMP AND GRITS

PERFECT STRANGERS AT THE PERFECT TIME

A random act of kindness by a complete stranger changed my life and was the impetus for my book *One Simple Act: Discovering the Power of Generosity.* I told the story in that book, but I need to tell it again here.

After a long trip I was heading back to Seattle. I had gotten up at three in the morning to catch a car to Newark Airport. As I arrived at my gate, I noticed that the Starbucks had just opened. Immediately a long line formed as caffeine-starved travelers sought relief. I patiently waited my turn and was rewarded with my favorite vanilla fat-free latte. I couldn't wait to get settled so I could take that first sip. The anticipation is always half the pleasure. Coffee at last. I juggled my purse, my knitting bag, and my carry-on into my chair. While I was putting everything down, wouldn't you know it, the latte slipped from my hand and tumbled onto the carpet. The entire latte spilled out. First of all, it was highly embarrassing, as everyone at the gate stared in my direction, and second, I wasn't about to stand in the line again because I'd been so incredibly clumsy. I wanted to kick myself.

I didn't feel I could leave the mess so I picked up a thick wad of napkins. The last thing I wanted was to bend over and expose the least favorite part of my anatomy to everybody. So I did the next best thing. I papered the carpet with napkins and did a little dance, stomping on the covered area in an attempt to blot up the latte. Of course, every eye in the gate area watched my every move. And it wasn't just one gate area. There happened to be three gates, packed full, that all converged on this spot.

When I had soaked up the liquid as best I could, I picked up the cup and soppy napkins and put the whole mess in the garbage. I then sat down, trying to be invisible.

As I settled in and reached for my knitting, a businessman came by and said, "You know, I'm going to go get myself a cup of coffee. May I get you something?"

What a generous gesture. "That's so nice. Here let me pay you." I reached for my purse.

He shook his head. "No, this is my good deed for the day." And he went and got me a latte.

That simple act of kindness had a profound effect on me — that somebody would be that kind. I felt good about it all day. Since that time I have made the effort to practice doing a good deed every single day. A stranger's act completely changed my life and has boomeranged into untold "good deeds" done by those who've read *One Simple Act.*

Gifts from Our Guests: An unexpected act of kindness from a stranger, offered when we least expect it, can become a springboard from which our own kindness can leap into the lives of others. Such acts are like little hugs from God.

A Congressman's Compassion

Congressman Elijah E. Cummings of Maryland's Seventh Congressional District tells of the Mother's Day he will never forget, a day when God called him to the side of a stranger. Here's his story:

The Saturday before Mother's Day began as an ordinary day for me. That afternoon, returning home from buying some flowers for the occasion, I stopped on Route 40 to fill my gas tank at Carroll Fuel.

As I drove into the filling station, I was startled to see a young man lying on the pavement, struggling to get up. Again and again, he would try to rise — but each time, he would fall back. In horror, I realized that blood was gushing from his chest with each attempt. The blood seemed to be going everywhere.

As I jumped from my car, I could hear four or five women screaming into their cell phones for an ambulance. I ran to the young man and knelt by his side to see if I could help him. I knew that we had to find a way to slow his bleeding. As gently as I could, I helped him turn over on his back and held his head on my arm.

I told him to remain calm — and assured him that I would wait with him until an ambulance arrived. We were strangers, but the young man seemed to recognize that I was trying to help. Yet, despite my pleas, he continued his struggle to rise.

After a few moments, I realized that he might not understand what I was trying to say to him. I fumbled in my pocket, found my cell phone, and dialed a friend who speaks Spanish. "How do you say 'Stay down!' " I pleaded into the phone. "How do you say, 'It's going to be allright?' "

The young man kept gasping for air — a struggle for life that was so intense, it took my own breath away — and the minutes that followed seemed like hours. We may have begun as strangers, but we were trapped together in the slow motion of a terrifying dream. Although there were other people nearby, it seemed as if the young man and I were the only two people in the world.

Life cried out to life, there on that concrete pavement, trying desperately to be understood. I kept trying to comfort the young stranger and slow his bleeding. Over and over, I repeated the calming Spanish words that I had just learned, cradling his head in my arms and praying for him.

It seemed as if his life was slipping away, and I felt a profound sense of sadness. When he heard me say the word "Jesus," he squeezed my hand.

Finally, a Baltimore County police officer appeared, kneeling beside us. Together, she and I were able to remove the young man's shirt, exposing his chest and his terrible knife wounds.

An emergency medical team soon followed to drive him to a hospital. When the ambulance was gone, I knew that this young man and I had shared a moment that was very deep and personal — and I realized that I did not even know his name.

Later, from the news reports, I learned that Carlos Santay-Carillo had not survived. I also learned that his wife, Claudia, had been in labor, preparing to give birth to their son, even as Carlos lay dying. He had come to the gas station that afternoon to buy fuel so that he could drive his wife to the hospital. Fate had carried me to the same place just moments after Carlos was attacked.

On Mother's Day weekend 2008, a father died in a Baltimore hospital, far from his native Guatemala. At almost the same moment as his death, his son, also named Carlos, was born healthy and sound in another hospital nearby.

In those moments, a new life — eyes not yet opened to the promise and pain that is our America — became our countryman. I may never come to know him, but at least I will know his name.

Gifts from Our Guests: Sometimes we are mystified by encounters God brings our way, but we realize that, in an instant, we connected eye to eye, during a momentous life event, and saw life through the eyes of another. And we come away the richer for it.

Seed Money for a Magic Waiter

I'm glad God sent radio personality Rhett Palmer into my life. He's definitely on my list. Aside from being one of those affable, bigger-than-life people, Rhett has the gift of being able to focus in on the people around him. He's one of the most popular radio hosts in central Florida, but it's not just his on-air personality that makes him so. When Wayne and I are out with Rhett, no matter where we go, it seems half the world knows him. And before the night is over, he somehow manages to connect with the other half. They call him the Mayor of the Airwaves, but a politician could only dream of Rhett's kind of popularity. In this chapter I'm talking about strangers who come into our lives, but Rhett doesn't allow people to remain strangers for long.

I met Rhett in the most unlikely way. Wayne first began listening to him on the radio. One day on the spur of the moment

Wayne picked up the phone and called the station. Without following the protocol a publicist uses — things like first sending a press kit or biography — Wayne just opened with "You need to interview my wife." Can you imagine? The normal celebrity interviewer would hear something like that and dismiss it immediately. Not Rhett. He dug right in and started asking Wayne questions. Rhett sees potential in every person he meets.

One night while eating dinner at the Steak 'n' Shake, Rhett managed to find out that the waiter was an aspiring magician. True to form, Rhett pressed him to do a couple of tricks.

"You are really good at this," Rhett told him.

The young man beamed. "I wish I could make a living at it."

"All you need to get started is a few business cards and a website," Rhett advised. "Once people see you perform and know how to get in touch with you, then you can start booking events."

"Unfortunately that takes money — all the more reason to get back to work."

When dinner was over, Rhett took a hundred-dollar bill out of his wallet and handed it to the waiter. "I believe in you.

Use this as seed money to get started on your dream."

A couple of years later that same young man phoned Rhett to thank him. He said that Rhett's belief in him had spurred him forward. He proudly announced that he was now earning his living entertaining people with his magic tricks. Sometimes it only takes a nudge in the right direction — even from a perfect stranger — for people to follow their dreams.

Gifts from Our Guests: Strangers often show up in our lives with gifts at divine moments. Their words or acts of encouragement — out of the blue — may be exactly what we need to hear.

Shrimp and Grits

Because I am a self-confessed foodie, some of the most welcome strangers in my life are chefs. I appreciate the art of cooking. I have to laugh at the number of times, while doing television appearances, that I've met chefs as fellow guests waiting in the greenrooms with me. But I'm not complaining.

Last fall when I was in Knoxville, I met chef Tory McPhail of New Orleans' famous Commander's Palace. That's the restaurant that was home to Paul Prudhomme, Emeril

Lagasse, and the late Jamie Shannon. Chef McPhail was cooking there during Hurricane Katrina, and did he ever have stories to tell! A huge oak tree fell on Commander's Palace, so it was closed for thirteen months. You'd think a chef of his standing would fall back on insurance, taking the year off. Not Tory McPhail. He used the time to develop a cookbook, *Commander's Wild Side.* I've thought about that kind of work ethic when it comes to channeling our creativity. Instead of letting an unforeseen event derail our dreams, we can just do what chef Tory McPhail did — pack up our "knives" and create something brand-new.

It's been fun for me to meet these chefs, especially since I've started writing cookbooks of my own. When I was in New Orleans doing a TV show, the producers had booked another chef as a guest, Wayne Baquet from Li'l Dizzy's Café. Chef Wayne's family boasts more than two hundred years of New Orleans history, and he's the third generation in the restaurant business. Li'l Dizzy's is located in an old bank building complete with vault and teller windows. Wayne's known for his authentic gumbo, but on the show he began talking about his shrimp and grits — a southern specialty. I couldn't stop thinking about shrimp and grits — one of my favorites — so my editor, Paula Eykelhof, and I set out for Li'l Dizzy's for breakfast. Chef Wayne came out of the kitchen and sat down and visited with us. He may have started out a stranger, but when someone cooks for me — food from his heart — I have to wonder if they aren't on my guest list as the kind of people God sends into my life to simply bring joy.

Gifts from Our Guests: The simple joys brought by strangers who show up on our guest lists remind us that God delights in pleasing His children.

When we become aware of all the Lord is doing in our lives through others, we will want to be sure to pay attention to the strangers God sends our way. I'm surprised by how many times a stranger is there to say or do exactly what is needed.

I often jot down funny things people have said to me or write about encounters that seem . . . well . . . divine. I love going back to discover instance after instance of God's hand at work through people I might not have noticed had I not been paying attention.

It's made me more aware of the people who cross my path. I recently heard a CEO speak about his interview protocol. He said that when hiring for executive positions, he always arranges to take the candidate to lunch. It's not just for the chance to get to know that candidate on a social level. It's actually a test. He watches how the candidate treats the waitstaff. He has discovered that those who are rude, condescending, or dismissive of those serving never make good executives. Interesting. We never know who is watching how we treat strangers. But we do know that God is watching.

I want to live in such a way that I can be God's invited guest on someone else's guest list, even that of a stranger. Here are some of the ways we can do that, often without their even being aware:

- Pray for people we see on the street, in airports, or at a meeting. Just right then and there, we can silently talk to God about them. It's one of the ways we can affect people's lives without intruding in any way. When I see a young mom struggling with her child or a person having trouble physically, I pray, asking God to intervene and ease the person's burden.
- Find a "safe" way to give. I struggle with giving money to obviously needy people I meet on the street. We all worry about enabling substance abuse, but I like what a friend of mine does. She carries fast-food gift cards with her and gives those, making sure that the stranger can at least get a hot meal.
- A simple courtesy can go a long way, much like the complimentary cup of coffee offered to me by the man at the airport. We can open a door, pick up a dropped item, offer a seat, give a

compliment.

- A smile costs absolutely nothing, and sometimes it is all that is needed to connect with a stranger.

We need to remember that we are often the hands or feet of Jesus to other people, whether we know them or not. Just as we strive to be aware of the strangers on our own guest lists, we need to be alert to the invitations God may issue to us to be that stranger in someone else's life.

*The people to whom I am sending you
are obstinate and stubborn.*
— EZEKIEL 2:4

FIVE:
TULIPS,
THE SELF-APPOINTED CRITIC,
AND CARRY-ON LUGGAGE

PRICKLY PEOPLE

My friend's daughter used to answer every comment with the pseudodefensive retort "Are you calling me fat?" It was so funny. A person might say, "Mandy, are you having dinner with us?" and she'd reply with her signature line. The reason it was so funny was that, though Mandy was teasing, we all know people who react this way. I call them prickly people.

There are shelves of books written about prickly people — how to get along with them in the workplace, how to get them to do what needs to be done, how to avoid their toxicity. I want to address it from a different angle. I want to suggest that sometimes God has placed those porcupine-like people on our guest lists for His very special purposes.

I had one of those prickly people in my life. When I first moved my office out of my home, I knew I needed a secretary —

someone to deal with the business details of my writing career so I could be free to write books and take care of my readers. I went through two assistants in quick order. The first one quit, and the second one spent her day making long-distance phone calls and charging them to the office. She couldn't get her office work done but managed to finish book after book of crossword puzzles on the job. I had to let her go. After that, I set out to find just the right person for the job. This time it happened to be a man. It had to go better this time, right? It certainly couldn't get worse, could it?

I never should have asked that question. It got a whole lot worse. My new assistant was a take-charge kind of guy. He had been administrative assistant for an up-and-coming politician. He tried very hard not to be disdainful of working for what he considered a "romance writer," but no matter how hard he tried, he couldn't hide his distaste.

He believed it was his job to whip my life into shape. He had no children, but he felt he knew best how Wayne and I should raise our children. When the kids would call, he'd often give them advice or refuse to put them through. He gave me direction on everything from what to eat to where to shop.

And he was prickly not only to me. He

would slam the phone down on my agent, saying, "Debbie's writing. She can't be interrupted now."

I have to admit I was stymied. Because the first two assistants hadn't worked out, I was determined to make this work. I kept worrying that the trouble was with me. Every now and then I'd screw up my courage and try to have a heart-to-heart with him. Because I was nervous, however, I would have a hard time explaining myself. I'd stammer and grope for the correct word. One time he slammed his fist down on the desk, and said, "If you can't talk, how do you expect to write?"

Another time, after a particularly bad day, I asked, "Do you want to continue to work for me?"

He responded, "If I work for you, I want it understood I will not be your friend." The next day he came back with a list of demands he insisted be met if he were to continue to be my assistant. Demands. I somehow stiffened my spine and told him that since I'd not be able to meet his demands, we'd best part ways. It was one of the happiest days of my career.

I said that sometimes God brings these prickly people into our lives. In this case, I believe it was important for me to learn to take control of my office. Had he not come into my life, I might have continued to abdicate responsibility in the face of a stronger personality.

And more than that, having him sitting at that desk made me appreciate the most wonderful assistant ever — Renate Roth — who's now been with me over fifteen years.

Gifts from Our Guests: Sometimes the prickly person's gift is just a challenge to be stronger.

Tulips for Another Spring

Fellow writer T. Suzanne Eller tells about a prickly person in her life whom she will never forget:

Jack tossed the papers on my desk — his eyebrows knit into a straight line as he glared at me.

"What's wrong?" I asked.

He jabbed a finger at the proposal. "Next time you want to change anything, ask me first," he said, turning on his heels and leaving me stewing in anger.

How dare he treat me like that, I thought. I had changed one long sentence, and corrected grammar — something I thought I was paid to do.

It's not that I hadn't been warned. The other women who had served in my place before me called him names I couldn't repeat. One co-worker took me aside the first day. "He's personally responsible for two different secretaries leaving the firm," she whispered.

As the weeks went by, I grew to despise Jack. It was against everything I believed in — turn the other cheek and love your enemies. But Jack quickly slapped a verbal insult on any cheek turned his way. I prayed about it, but to be honest, I wanted to put him in his place, not love him.

One day, another of his episodes left me in tears. I stormed into his office, prepared to lose my job if needed, but not before I let the man know how I felt. I opened the door and Jack glanced up.

"What?" he said abruptly.

Suddenly I knew what I had to do. After all, he deserved it.

I sat across from him. "Jack, the way you've been treating me is wrong. I've never had anyone speak to me that way. As a professional, it's wrong, and it's wrong for me to allow it to continue," I said.

Jack snickered nervously and leaned back in his chair. I closed my eyes briefly. God help me, I prayed.

"I want to make you a promise. I will be a friend," I said. "I will treat you as you deserve to be treated, with respect and kindness. You deserve that," I said. "Everybody does." I slipped out of the chair and closed the door behind me.

Jack avoided me the rest of the week. Proposals, specs, and letters appeared on my desk while I was at lunch, and the corrected versions were not seen again. I brought cookies to the office one day and left a batch on Jack's desk. Another day I left a note. "Hope your day is going great," it read.

Over the next few weeks, Jack re-appeared. He was reserved, but there were no other episodes. Co-workers cornered me in the break room.

"Guess you got to Jack," they said. "You must have told him off good." I shook my head.

"Jack and I are becoming friends," I said in faith. I refused to talk about him. Every time I saw Jack in the hall, I smiled at him.

After all, that's what friends do.

One year after our "talk," I discovered

I had breast cancer. I was 32, the mother of three beautiful young children, and scared. The cancer had metastasized to my lymph nodes and the statistics were not great for long-term survival. After surgery, I visited with friends and loved ones who tried to find the right words to say. No one knew what to say. Many said the wrong things. Others wept, and I tried to encourage them. I clung to hope.

The last day of my hospital stay, the door darkened and Jack stood awkwardly on the threshold. I waved him in with a smile and he walked over to my bed and, without a word, placed a bundle beside me. Inside lay several bulbs.

"Tulips," he said.

I smiled, not understanding.

He cleared his throat. "If you plant them when you get home, they'll come up next spring." He shuffled his feet. "I just wanted you to know that I think you'll be there to see them when they come up."

Tears clouded my eyes and I reached out my hand.

"Thank you," I whispered.

Jack grasped my hand and gruffly replied, "You're welcome. You can't see it now, but next spring you'll see the colors I picked out for you." He turned and left without a word.

I have seen those red-and-white-striped tulips push through the soil every spring for over ten years now. In fact, this September the doctor will declare me cured. I've seen my children graduate from high school and enter college.

In a moment when I prayed for just the right word, a man with very few words said all the right things.

After all, that's what friends do.

Gifts from Our Guests: A person's prickly exterior may be masking an inability to connect — a social ineptness. It doesn't mean he or she doesn't bring a gift into our lives. We may need to look harder or wait longer for the gift, but when it comes, it's especially precious.

The Self-appointed Critic

One of the challenges of being a writer is dealing with the critics. I've been blessed in my career to have suffered little at the hands of critics. Until, that is, I began to write of my faith. Some of the criticism blindsided me. Believe it or not, most of the censure I received came from Christians. I've even received letters that said: "How can you call yourself a Christian? I'm writing the publisher, and I'm telling them I will never buy it again if they publish you." Yikes!

What did I do wrong? Sometimes, perhaps, it's just that my way of talking about my faith doesn't sound like the reader's way of describing his or her faith. Other times readers have picked up one of my earlier books, which are regularly being reissued, and found an offensive scene in it. I have been writing for a long time as my faith has been deepening. In my stories themselves, if the characters had premarital sex, there were always consequences to it. I never wanted to glorify that relationship outside of marriage. They may have sensual moments, but never premarital sex without complications, and very, very few of those scenes at that. And the books I write now are altogether different from when I first wrote romance. They are women's fiction — more about relationships than romance. But very often they all end up on the shelf together.

I've realized there's not much I can do to change those earlier books that some readers find offensive. However, I respond to the person I've offended by explaining that I am nothing without the grace of Jesus Christ. One reader wrote me to tell me she regretted the money she spent on a certain book. I offered to make a donation equal to the price of the book and send it to her favorite charity. In her return letter she opened her heart to me — writing a long letter about losing her thirty-four-year-old grandson to complications of diabetes. He was alone in a hotel room and suffered a heart attack — all due to diabetes. She said it would mean the world to her if I would make a donation to the diabetes foundation so that they could find a cure. We moved from her prickly original letter to working together to fight a tragic disease — all because I'd responded to her letter with love and she responded back to me in kind.

I've gotten initial letters saying, "I'll never buy anything you write again. How can you call yourself a Christian?" and then received a return letter saying, "Well, I serve a God of second chances. I'm willing to give you one, too."

So I've come to the conclusion that as a published author who doesn't own the rights to her earlier books, there's nothing I can do but lovingly answer the criticism and explain it the best I can. I'm so glad God offers us second chances and readers do as well.

Gifts from Our Guests: It took me a while to realize that criticism can be a gift, especially when it is the starting point of a conversation. From that interaction, a bond can be forged.

Cranky People

Sometimes I wonder if God doesn't put cranky people on my list, at least temporarily, for me to remember to keep things in perspective. Our ever-more-complicated world seems to cultivate crankiness. For instance, can you remember far enough back to when flying was a genteel way of travel? I do. I remember when women carefully dressed in a travel suit and heels and carried beautiful overnight cases. They would kiss their loved ones good-bye at the gate and step onto the plane, slipping their cases under the seat in front of them. Young stewardesses who were still excited about their glamorous vocation would welcome them. After greeting their seatmates, they would settle in for a relaxing flight.

It's no wonder we are crankier these days. We get to the airport and are hustled out of the car with our suitcases while security waves our ride away. We grapple with our luggage and have to check ourselves in at a kiosk and manhandle our own luggage over to security. We can't take water or liquids to our departure gate, so we check our bags and throw away our lotions and drinks. We're juggling carry-on bags and heavy computer cases.

To get through security, we practically have to undress and wait in a long line while the guy ahead of us forgets to get his change out of his pocket. We're momentarily relieved that our airport hasn't yet installed full-body scans. At the end, if we don't have to be patted down or rescreened, we get to re-dress and try to stow everything back into our carry-ons.

By the time we get to the gate, our nerves are frazzled. We then watch the board to make sure there are no delays or maintenance issues, overbooking, or gate changes. When we finally board, it's a mad scramble to find room for our carry-on luggage because it seems as if everyone has somehow managed to carry all their household goods onto the plane. The seats are smaller than ever, and legroom is practically nonexistent. Every seat is taken, and as the entire planeful of people manages to squeeze into position, cranky voices are raised over the din. It's no wonder we've coined a new term — air rage.

Much of the crankiness of our age is

caused by an ever-creeping loss of gentility. We have more and more regulations, we do more in less time, everything is self-service, and most of us are pushed to the limit. Do you remember when gas station attendants came out to greet us with a smile, pump our gas, check under our hoods, and speed us on our way? That's been replaced with yet another task for us to do. And those who used to do that job are out of work and worrying about how to put food on the table.

So what can we do about it? Well, I don't know how to begin to change the system, but since God may have called these cranky people into my life for a time, I try to let my attitude defuse the tension. I take my action plan from the love chapter in the Bible: "Love is patient, love is kind. It does not envy, it does not boast, it is not proud. It is not rude, it is not self-seeking, it is not easily angered, it keeps no record of wrongs. Love does not delight in evil but rejoices with the truth. It always protects, always trusts, always hopes, always perseveres" (1 Corinthians 13:4–7).

It's like a magic formula. Apply it to any situation, and improvement begins almost immediately. Think about what the world would be like if we all used this as a guideline — never rude, always kind, patient . . .

We would have heaven on earth.

Gifts from Our Guests: Cranky people often offer us the gift of a fresh opportunity to develop patience.

I'm not sure that I want to suggest you keep a journal of the prickly people in your life. This is one of the few instances in this book when we need to take the attitude "It is what it is." Verse 5 in the above passage from the love chapter in 1 Corinthians says, "Love keeps no record of wrongs." The last thing we want to do is write all those wrongs down to be examined later.

I've heard prickly people called sandpaper people. If we want to focus on these guests in our lives, let's focus on how they've made us smoother — how they've sanded off some of the rough places in our lives.

Our secret weapon is love. If we can continue to cultivate love toward the prickly people in our lives, we'll have less and less to write down. The last verse in the love chapter says it best: "And now these three remain: faith, hope and love. But the greatest of these is love" (1 Corinthians 13:13).

RSVP

I'm hoping we don't become the prickly people on someone else's guest list. There's no doubt we will have times of being out of sorts and cranky, but that's not the same thing as being a chronically difficult person. If you are in danger of sinking into a permanent porcupine-like state, consider doing the following:

- Figure out what's bothering you, and work to resolve it. This sounds easier than it is. Sometimes we need help — even professional help — to do this.
- Take care of the physical. Are you getting enough sleep? Do you eat right? Do you need to see a doctor?
- Reduce the stress. We all live under a load of stress. Be creative and try to find ways to minimize that stress.
- Apply discipline to the situation. Even though I may feel out of sorts or permanently cranky, I don't have to let anyone else see that. If I use the guidelines in the love chapter (1 Corinthians 13) and try to avoid rudeness, instead being patient and kind, I can change the dynamic. When we resolve to discipline ourselves to practice this kind of

response, very often we find that the feelings will follow.

I will sing of the LORD's great love forever; with my mouth I will make your faithfulness known through all generations.

— PSALM 89:1

Six:
A Faded Letter,
Autographs, and the
Prayers of an Unknown
Mother-in-law

THE WISDOM OF DEAD PEOPLE

It might seem odd to have a chapter on dead people, but those who've gone before us are often invited by God to be part of our lives. My friend Wendy Lawton wrote the following story about finding a letter from her long-deceased great-grandmother:

Who would have guessed from looking at the water-stained pasteboard box that it contained a priceless treasure? As I examined the faded family photographs, a brittle piece of lined paper dropped to the floor. The script was faint, but I read the words of her handwritten prayer — "This day, July 10, 1912, I hereby sign and give my son Robert over to the Lord, for the Lord to redeem his soul from sin and to make him an earnest Christian . . ." Suddenly, a shared faith connected me to a great-grandmother I had never met.

I had discovered something more valuable than gold — a footprint of faith in a family that had seemed singularly godless. My father faintly remembered his grandmother, Elizabeth McKelvey Coats, as a godly woman, but this scrap of paper confirmed it.

Elizabeth Coats was a woman of vibrant faith. Her prayer, committing her thirty-five-year-old son into the hands of the Lord, communicated a vital witness. The act of relinquishment and the faith that it embodies speaks across the years. My great-uncle Robert chose to live his life without acknowledging the God of his mother. Indeed, each of Elizabeth Coats' children fell away from the Lord. But God honors prayer in ways we often don't expect, and He honored my great-grandmother's prayer on behalf of generations she never met.

My grandmother, Elizabeth Coats' youngest daughter, married into a Jewish family and my father was raised with one foot in the synagogue and the other in nominal Protestantism. He chose neither.

As I was growing up, my mother faithfully took my brother, sisters and me to Sunday school and church even though my father didn't attend. One Sunday, when she couldn't go, my father dropped us off. That morning I heard the plan of salvation so clearly, that at the age of seven, I asked Jesus to come into my heart. The Lord accepted that childish request and the repentance that came with it. Our Children's Church leader asked me to stay after church to talk. My father, who had come to pick us up, patiently waited and afterward, listened to all I had to tell him. Three years later my father, Elizabeth Coats' beloved grandson, found Christ. He served the Lord with enthusiasm and energy for the remaining seven years of his life.

Years later when I found my great-grandmother's prayer, I affirmed a milestone on our family's spiritual journey. Just as the Jews of the Scriptures recalled God's faithfulness generation to generation, our family story reminds us that the Lord keeps renewing his covenant.

Gifts from Our Guests: Family faith stories bring the gift of a spiritual legacy that can be passed down through the generations.

Autographs

There are so many authors — all long gone now — who affected my life. I knew they were on God's guest list for my life, but I longed to have something tangible from them — some kind of memento. I decided to collect their autographs. The first autograph I bought was Catherine Marshall's because I loved her book *Christy* so much. I read it and treasured every word. It helped birth the dream that I could actually write a book someday.

To hold her autograph was just amazing to me. In fact, when it came, I wept with joy. Her handwriting is so beautiful, and it came framed with her husband, Peter Marshall's, autograph. He was a U.S. chaplain, and his is such a phenomenal story. I was so excited, I called my friend Linda and said, "I've got my autograph of —" Unfortunately I was so excited and talking so fast I couldn't get the name out. Linda, who's not the sentimental type, finally said, "Well, *whose autograph* did you get? Jesus'?"

So Catherine Marshall's was the very first autograph I bought. After I hung it up in my home, I started thinking about all the other authors whose books affected me. When I was a child, I loved Willa Cather's books of life on the prairie. They felt autobiographical to me because my parents came from the prairie land — the Badlands, really — of the Dakotas. So I got Willa Cather's, and then I got Edna Ferber's, who was another author I devoured. I read every Cather and Ferber book the library could unearth. They helped shape me as a writer. I wanted to tell those kinds of engaging stories.

I read Rudyard Kipling in a literature class and was in awe of his ability to write short stories. I remember when I got his signature, it came with a photograph of more than one person, but I didn't know which one was Rudyard Kipling. So I called the dealer to ask. He said, "My dear, the man on the left is King George." Like I should know.

Then I started collecting in earnest. Those first ones started my passion for finding authors' autographs. I wanted Ernest Hemingway's because of the short story that he wrote called "The Short Happy Life of Francis Macomber." It was the first time Macomber had turned up in any kind of fiction that I knew of. I added Charles Dickens's because I wanted to have my stories read and treasured and loved as much as his. And Mark Twain's for the same reason. I collected Harriet Beecher Stowe's because I loved her faith in action and

113

because *Uncle Tom's Cabin* was a novel that changed history.

I read *Seventeen* by Booth Tarkington when I was young, and so I collected his signature. I admire the wit of E. E. Cummings, and so I got his signature. It became such a joy to find them. The search was half the fun. I travel so much that every time I came to a new town, I'd go to the hotel and look in the yellow pages for autograph dealers. If one was anywhere close to the hotel, I would go to that autograph studio and spend hours looking at their stock, like a kid in a candy shop. I now have over fifty autographs in my collection.

As I write each day, I look at all those autographs framed on the walls of my office. They speak to the power of story and the influence those writers have had on society. Being surrounded by these literary giants made me think more deeply about the stories I wanted to write. I long to write stories that are relevant, stories that are provocative, stories that touch hearts, and stories that shine the light on the pathway to God. Those writers — long gone now — are my mentors, my heroes.

Gifts from Our Guests: Sometimes having a tangible memento of our heroes — the gift of a little scrap of their lives — helps us to keep them in our sights.

A Literary Pilgrimage

Brian T. Carroll is someone who welcomes the influence of what the Bible calls that "great cloud of witnesses" (Hebrews 12:1) in his life. Here's what he wrote in a comment posted to a blog:

One of my favorite literary genres is missionary diaries and memoir, the more obscure and remote the better. I guess we each escape to our own Neverland. One of my favorites is the diary of Samuel Pollard, an Englishman who served in Yunnan, China, 1880s to 1914. He saw 4,000 Miao (Hmong) come to Christ. I visited China in 2004 and asked some Chinese friends to accompany me to Zhaotong, Pollard's outpost. They complained that it held nothing of interest to tourists, but we went.

Local officials gave us a tour of the hospital, school, church, and seminary founded by Pollard, all still vibrant after half a century of communism. Then they gave me a copy of Pollard's translation of the New Testament, now rendered obsolete by a new alphabet. I was not allowed into the adobe building where Pollard had lived and worked, because they feared the building was close to collapse. A few hours after we left, a major earthquake left 120,000 homeless in Zhaotong. I may have visited Pollard's headquarters on the last day it stood. Or seen another way, God may have left the building upright just long enough for me to stand beside it and picture the events in Pollard's diary. Once I'd seen it, God let it return to the dust from which it had come.

Gifts from Our Guests: There is something about visiting the stomping grounds of our heroes that brings the gift of understanding them into context for us.

A Mother-in-law's Prayers

Kelly, a friend of mine, was speaking at a women's retreat about the importance of discovering your family's legacy of faith. The first weekend she delivered her message, it was well received. When she repeated it the second weekend, several of the ladies asked her what they could do if they came from dysfunctional families. What if there was no legacy of faith to pass on? It was a valid question. The meeting planner suggested that Kelly gather several of those women together to talk.

As they began to talk, the stories became bleaker. Kelly, who came from a healthy, loving family, wondered where God was in all this.

One woman — I'll call her Mary — spoke up and asked if she could tell her story. She said her circumstances were not much different from the others'. Most nights while she was a young girl her bedroom door would open and her own father would enter in the dark to abuse her. Mary said she was always somehow able to blank it out. During counseling, her counselor had been curious as to why it had not affected her as profoundly as it often affects victims. Kelly said the others in the room were curious as well. "When I got married," Mary said, "my husband's mother was already dead. I never got to meet her, but my husband let me read her journals. As I opened journal after journal, I read her prayers for me — a daughter-in-law she never met. Night after night, she would pray for her son's future wife — that God would protect her and keep her safe." Mary continued, "I looked at the dates and realized that she was covering me with prayer on those awful nights. God didn't stop the abuse at that point, but

I believe to this day that the prayers of my husband's mother somehow protected me from the worst of the damage."

Gifts from Our Guest: The gift of prayer is not hampered by earthly constraints. Isn't it uncanny that a relationship can be forged that transcends our normal bounds of time and place and a guest no longer living can still bring us a gift?

TAKE NOTE

Just as I treasure my autograph collection, think about ways you can gather the wisdom of the people who've been called into your life. Madeleine L'Engle, in her wonderful book *Walking on Water,* talks about keeping her Commonplace Book. She says it was a big brown Mexican notebook. Over the years she copied down words that captivated her, passages from books, and sayings of those who had touched her life. She says, "All I'm looking for in it is meaning, meaning which will help me live life lovingly."

I love the idea of a Commonplace Book with quotes and clips and sketches — just filled with wisdom.

I've got a friend who collects books. Her shelves are filled with books written by her spiritual mentors — C. S. Lewis, Henri Nouwen, Dorothy L. Sayers, G. K. Chesterton, Madeleine L'Engle, George Mac-Donald, and others.

However you choose to gather the gifts left behind, don't let that legacy of wisdom slip through your fingers.

RSVP

We don't like to think of what we'll leave behind after we are gone, but my friend Wendy Lawton, in her article called "Footprints of Faith," suggested several ways to leave a record of your spiritual journey. Here are some of her suggestions to help you find a natural expression of your faith:

- Take notes in your Bible and in the books you read. Besides the value of these notations for your own study, the markings become a record of your journey. Wouldn't you cherish an ancestor's Bible with notes and underlinings, thoughts and prayers, favorite verses and spiritual insights? As a book collector, I know the value of books purchased from the libraries of the faithful. The notes are often as insightful as the text. It's a simple and natural way to leave a footprint of faith.

- Journaling is a powerful way to chronicle your faith. Historians cull much of the immediacy and color of an era from first-person accounts. In the same way, family members will benefit from seeing the mountains and valleys of your spiritual journey. You need a willingness to be vulnerable.

No one wants to read a fictional account of the exemplary life. The value and strength of a memoir come in the simplicity of truth, warts and all.

- Correspondence makes a lasting impact. Ignore the convenience of the telephone and return to pen and paper for important family correspondence. We tend to save letters. As the years pass, they become more precious. Commemorate important milestones like births, deaths, graduations, and marriages with letters expressing what the recipient means to you and what you appreciate most about them.

- Family recipes are rich with sensory remembrance. Compile a recipe file, but include more than just the ingredients. Add family memories. Gather a collection of meaningful prayers of thanks — your own "grace" notes. Include appropriate verses and poems. Churches publish spiral-bound cookbooks to raise funds, little realizing that with the passage of time, these become treasured remembrances of the hospitality and creativity of those who have gone to be with the Lord.

- Keep a family hymnal and make liberal notations in the margins. "Rebecca sang this for morning worship on June 15, 1995"; "sung at Grandma's funeral by Emil Olson"; or just "Mama's favorite hymn — I can remember her singing in full voice while hanging out the wash."

- Do you draw, paint, or sculpt? Your creative works bear witness to your faith long after you are gone. Creative gifts often point to the Creator more clearly than spoken words. A poem, prayerfully written, draws us into the presence of the Lord. A garden bears witness to the gardener's faith, through the notes, records, and anecdotes the gardener keeps.

Your life of faith will leave a trail of stories and memories in your wake. Our desire should be that we will be remembered, not for who we were or what we did, but for whom we lived.

*And to think you were
midwife at my birth,
setting me at my mother's breasts!
When I left the womb you cradled me;
since the moment of birth
you've been my God.*
— PSALM 22:9–10 (THE MESSAGE)

SEVEN:
THE FULL RECTORY,
AN IMPERFECT DAUGHTER,
AND AN ANGEL MOTHER

EVEN BEFORE I WAS BORN

Had Susanna Wesley lived today, she might have been dismissed as a poor stay-at-home mother of an inordinate number of children. But Susanna Wesley changed the world through her role as a mother.

She came from a large family herself. She was the twenty-fifth of twenty-five children born to a seventeenth-century English clergyman and his wife. She also married a clergyman, Samuel Wesley, and began caring for his household and welcoming babies into their family. In all, she had nineteen children, only ten of whom survived childhood.

The rectory was filled with children whom one contemporary scholar called "a cluster of bright, vehement, argumentative boys and girls, living by a clean and high code, and on the plainest fare; but drilled to soft tones, to pretty formal courtesies; with learning as an ideal, duty as an atmosphere and fear of God as law."

Susanna believed in God and in education. She schooled the children for six hours a day — the girls and boys alike. She set aside time in the evenings to spend alone with each child. During one of her husband's absences she wrote this in her diary:

I am a woman, but I am also the mistress of a large family. And though the superior charge of the souls contained in it lies upon you, yet in your long absence I cannot but look upon every soul you leave under my charge as a talent committed to me under a trust. I am not a man nor a minister, yet as a mother and a mistress I felt I ought to do more than I had yet done. I resolved to begin with my own children; in which I observe, the following method: I take such a proportion of time as I can spare every night to discourse with each child apart. On Monday I talk with Molly, on Tuesday with Hetty, Wednesday with Nancy, Thursday with Jacky, Friday with Patty, Saturday with Charles.

Later her son John, Thursday's child, would write about how important those times were to him.

The Wesleys suffered more than their share of adversity. Samuel Wesley possessed little business sense, and Susanna managed the limited resources of the often-impoverished family. Samuel ended up in debtor's prison twice, leaving Susanna alone to care for the household and the children. Once he and Susanna separated for a time over a political dispute. As Susanna said, she would apologize if she was wrong, but she felt to do so for expediency only would be a lie and thus a sin.

The rectory caught fire twice, the second time when John was only five. Susanna thought she had managed to get all the children out of the house, but as she looked back at the inferno, she saw John standing at an upstairs window. His rescuer managed to climb up to the window on the shoulders of another man and brought John unharmed to his mother's arms.

It hardly sounds like an idyllic home, but this mother loved her husband and loved her children. In an age when discipline was harsh, sometimes brutal, Susanna's philosophy was "strength guided by kindness." Susanna once wrote, "I am content to fill a little space if God be glorified."

After her death she became known as the Mother of Methodism, because two of her sons turned the once-apathetic Christian world upside down. John Wesley, the son plucked from the fire in the rectory, founded the Methodist movement. His brother Charles was also a clergyman in the movement and best known for his thousands of hymns, which are still loved today. Their brother Samuel, also a pastor, remained in the Anglican church, and a number of the children became educators. Susanna's successful offspring can be traced for generations. It's an impressive heritage for a woman who asked only to "fill a little space."

As we seek to discover God's guest list for our lives, I want us to look closest to home first. Our mothers may have been the very first person God sent into our lives.

The song "A Mother's Hands," written by Carolyn Scott Ahlem, suggests that God uses our mothers to be His hands:

Our Father, you speak to us in the
    silence.
You sing to us in the wind.
When we came to earth you were there
    at our birth,
Touching us first with a mother's hands.

You brighten the dark with the moon

and stars.
You warm our way with the sun.
When we were small and often would
    fall,
You lifted us up with a mother's hands.

Father we long to be close to you.
Sometimes you seem so far away.
And because you heed our every need,
You sent us your touch through a
    mother's hands.
We thank you, Lord, for a mother's
    hands.

Gifts from Our Guests: The gift of mothers is the gift of God's hands and feet meeting our most basic needs here on earth.

A Complicated Relationship

My relationship with my own mother was complicated. Mom was the oldest. My dad was the youngest boy in his large family. It made for an interesting combination. Mom grew up in a family where everybody worked. When she left Dickinson, North Dakota, to live in Yakima, Washington, she sent home as much of each paycheck as she could possibly manage, keeping only enough for her to survive. The rest went to support her parents and siblings. It was the Depression era, and they would have faced starvation if it were not for her.

Work became my mother's signature. For as long as I can remember, she rearranged the living room furniture once a month. Everything was meticulously clean. She scrubbed. She cleaned. I have her diary from World War II, and every day she would record how many hours she cleaned. Cleanliness was certainly next to godliness with her. Later, when it came to the grandkids, she'd "create memories" with them by cleaning.

"Let's do dishes," she'd say. "We're creating memories."

My mother's work ethic has become part of our family heritage, and I'm grateful for it. We all laughed on Thanksgiving when my daughter Jody gathered her kids and said, "Come on. We're making memories. Let's go do dishes."

I never was, and I never will be, the housekeeper my mother was. I'm afraid I was a disappointment to her when it came to housework.

Once when my daughter Jody was about five years old and saw me hauling the vacuum cleaner upstairs, she turned to me with her big innocent eyes and said, "Grandma coming?" Another time my mom and dad had driven three hours to come from Yakima to visit us in Seattle. My mother walked into the house, right past me, right past the kids, opened the microwave oven and said triumphantly, "I thought so!" And sure enough, it was dirty. She immediately got out a rag, a sponge, and a squirt bottle and got to it.

It was not just my housekeeping. I was a disappointment to my mother for most of my growing-up years. She started me in school early. They didn't have kindergarten at the school, so I started in the first grade. My birthday isn't until October, but she found a way to get me into first grade ahead of time. Unfortunately, classes had already been in session ten days before the school contacted Mom to say there was room for me after all. You can imagine how difficult that was. So here I was, the newcomer, and the first thing I did was walk into the boys' bathroom. I was mortified my very first day of school.

And it went downhill from there. When it came time to read, I found I just couldn't do it. No one understood or identified dyslexia in the early 1950s. And I didn't have many friends. My cousins were either several grades ahead of me or younger. There was another girl in the class who had trouble reading too. I befriended her because of our mutual struggle, but it wasn't long before she was placed in special education and left regular class. Once again I found myself friendless.

My mother, who valued hard work, couldn't understand why I couldn't apply myself to the task of reading. And because she had a wide circle of friends, she despaired of me when she realized I didn't have friends.

What's worse, I started gaining weight in the second and third grades. I was pudgy. I look back now and see that I wasn't that fat, but I always felt enormous. I look at a picture of me in the fifth grade, and I was already five-foot-one and weighed probably 120 pounds. I thought I was grotesquely obese.

My mother was a petite, beautiful woman. She would never step outside the house without meticulous hair and makeup. Her clothes were always the height of fashion. She had the most beautiful clothes. She was called the Jacqueline Kennedy of our family. Every year, she would work on getting a tan. She worked nights, and so she got up in the morning when my dad left for work and went outside to sleep in the sun so she could get a morning suntan.

And me? I was not smart and I was not beautiful.

As I said, my relationship with my mother was complicated. But I loved her and knew she loved me in spite of my shortcomings. So in trying to figure out who God has sent into my life — who is on my guest list — you might wonder why I'd include my mother. It's because so much of who I am came out of that complicated relationship.

I never became the housekeeper she was, but her need for order may very well be the reason I have such a highly developed sense of order. Mom's strong work ethic is one of the driving forces behind my career. I accomplish mountains of work due to organization and hard work. That came straight from my mother. I must admit, however, that when it comes to creating memories with my grandkids, I make sure those memories are something other than chores.

In addition to everything else, my mother was a phenomenal cook, very inventive, though she didn't have great self-confidence. I love to work in the kitchen as well, but I make sure not to let a lack of confidence hamper me. When I began to cook, I just got in there and experimented. My family still laughs about many of my experiments. At one point I was adding so many peppers to my recipes that Wayne had to gently remind me that food isn't supposed to hurt!

As I read my mother's diary, I came across an entry she made after she missed church one Sunday. She wrote, "God is going to punish me for sure." Oh, poor Mom. She was so close to God, but her religious upbringing was a fear-based love. She was always afraid she might do something to displease God. But despite that fear-tinged love, she longed for my brother and me to be close to God. She planted the deep desire in me to know Him. I have to thank God and my mother for that longing.

Because of my foundation in faith, I am close to God. As I matured in my faith, I learned that God loves me in a way that is not based on fear, but on relationship. There's real freedom in that. Freedom my mother didn't realize until the end of her life.

Powerful lessons.

My mother set the bar high when it came to generosity. Because she grew up in the time she did, and because she had to help support her family, the idea of helping others was so ingrained in her that it became a driving force in her life up until the day she died. I cannot remember a Christmas that she did not bake and cook for others. She would make platters and platters of cookies and candies to hand out to people. I can't remember my mother ever refusing people anything. If they needed it, my mother would bend over backward to help them in any way she could. If she had two of something, she made sure somebody else got the other. My book on giving, *One Simple Act,* grew out of my mother's legacy. I learned charity from watching her. She lived to help others.

As my mother grew older, we became incredibly close. I came to appreciate her for who she was, and she accepted me the way I am. As my writing career blossomed, I tried to involve my mother as much as possible. If I had a readers' group or a library gathering, I would always take her with me. She loved meeting the readers as much as I did. I would laugh to overhear her say things like, "Even as a child, Debbie was brilliant." I guess she forgot I barely made it from one grade to the next.

My mother is definitely on God's guest list for my life. I wouldn't be who I am without her. God knew what He was doing.

An Angel Mother

Abraham Lincoln also understood that God sent his mothers into his life. Yes, he had two mothers. His biological mother, Nancy Hanks Lincoln, died of milk fever when he was only ten years old. She'd grown up poor and gave birth to Abraham in a log cabin near Hodgenville, Kentucky. Not much is known about her except that she was an exceptional seamstress and her fine needlework was in high demand. Someone at the time wrote, "She was loved and revered by all who knew her." Of her, Abraham Lincoln said, "God bless my mother; all that I am or ever hope to be I owe to her."

Soon after Nancy Lincoln died, Abraham's father set off to find a new mother for his two children. He had known Sarah Bush Johnston, then a widow with three children, for many years. He paid off her husband's debts, settled the small family in his wagon, and headed back to Indiana, where the Lincolns had settled. It could have been a terrible situation for young Abraham and his sister — a Cinderella-like story with a wicked stepmother favoring her children over her stepchildren — but this godly woman never showed favoritism. She loved the Lincoln children from the moment she met them.

Thomas Lincoln, Abraham's father, never had much interest in books. He couldn't see why his son wanted to waste so much time reading. It was Abraham's stepmother who, while she herself was illiterate, pressed Abraham's father to let the boy read as much as he wanted. "Abe was the best boy I ever saw," she said of her stepson. "He never gave me a cross word or look." And Abraham loved his stepmother and called her "Mother." He always kept a forty-acre plot of land for "Mother while she lives."

We will never know what kind of man our beloved sixteenth president would have been had not these two mothers been on his list.

Gifts from Our Guests: Some mother gifts are far more complex than they first appear. Some inspire us to do great things; others are the sandpaper that rubs off a few rough spots so that the very best of who we are will shine.

Henry James said, "Journaling is a record of passing impressions that allows us to catch and keep something of life." We want to examine our lives, to savor those whom God has sent into our lives and to capture their influence and wisdom. One of the best ways we can do this is by journaling. If you are keeping a people journal, I suggest you have several pages for your mother. Make note of each memory you capture, and leave space to reflect. Don't be afraid to journal the troublesome memories as well as the good. Just as with my mother, those relationships can be complicated, but the more we chew on them, the more we'll come to understand.

If your mother is still with you, encourage her to write down her memories of you. In this day of video capture, I wish I had taken the time to videotape my mother reminiscing about her life and mine. How I'd like to go back and relive some of it through her eyes. There's much to learn about God's game plan for us by listening to those He sends into our lives.

RSVP

Just as God invited our mothers into our lives, we've been invited into our children's lives to influence them. This is true not only for those of us who are mothers, but for aunts, caregivers, and others of us who are entrusted with the nurturing of children.

Too often we hear, "I'm not going to be like my mother." That's valid. As we examine our mothers, we see that they were fallible, and we long to do better. Our mothers probably had the same wish. Truth is, we're going to be better in some ways, and in others, well, we may have a blind spot or two. Guess what our children will say?

I started daily devotions when I first became a Christian in 1972. Right away I set a pattern of getting up early, reading my Bible, and writing in my journal. So it just became a habit. I didn't do it to influence my children. In fact, I did it while they were all sleeping. But I can remember when the kids were in high school, they would stumble out of their rooms, find me in the kitchen, where I prayed, and say, "Mom, will you pray about . . ." And that always heartened me, that they knew they could go to their mother for prayer. So I think they received spiritual lessons more by example than by anything I said.

Our opportunity to influence our children does not end when they reach adulthood. We can have motherly influence on our children, no matter what their age. After all, God wrote us on their guest lists. The power of a mother, or motherlike relationship, lasts a lifetime. What can you do to make the most of this special God-given bond?

Listen, my son, to your father's instruction and do not forsake your mother's teaching.

— PROVERBS 1:8

EIGHT:
A STUFFED TEDDY,
A BREAD TRUCK, AND
A TIN BOX IN THE ATTIC
THE INFLUENCE OF A FATHER

From the time I can first remember, my father, Ted Adler, told stories. Just like his father before him. It's no wonder I grew up to be a storyteller. I can remember when I was about ten years old meeting some friends of my dad's. We spent a memorable day together, and before we left, one of them said, "You have your dad's personality." I remember how pleased I was to hear that, because my dad was always fun to be around. He had a multitude of friends, and he was a natural-born leader — which was exactly the way I wanted to be.

My dad was the youngest boy in a family of nine. By the time he came along, he needed a big, big personality in order to get attention. And that's exactly what he had. He was bigger than life, though in stature he was always small. At his tallest he probably only measured five foot five or five foot six. My dad's real name is not Ted. It's

Henry, but when he was a kid, he loved potatoes in any form. He loved them so much that when his older brother, my uncle A.D., passed down his vest to his little brother, my dad had such a big tummy that it pulled the buttons and stretched the buttonholes, and he looked like a well-stuffed, round-bellied teddy bear. That's how he got the name Teddy. And it stuck.

He was quite the character. Because his mother was diabetic and often sick, my aunt Betty practically raised my dad and his younger sister, my aunt Gerty. He insisted he was Betty's favorite, though. Aunt Betty, who, at the writing of this book, will celebrate her one hundredth birthday, is the only surviving member of all my father's brothers and sisters.

During the dust-bowl years, their farm failed. My grandparents lost everything — land, crops, and belongings. My dad's father packed up the Model A Ford with all they had left in the world and moved the family to Yakima, Washington, because they heard you could find work there picking fruit. Aunt Betty, grown by then, stayed behind, so she had to say goodbye to her little Teddy. She recently told me about the day she heard that Ted had been taken to the hospital with stomach pains. When the telegram came, she paced and worried until she finally broke down, found a telephone, and called. In those days of the Great Depression I can only imagine what it cost her to make that phone call to Yakima. Beside herself with worry, she listened to the whole story. My father had been taken to the hospital because they believed he was having an appendicitis attack. After much poking and prodding and some judicious questioning, the doctor discovered the cause of his discomfort: true to form, Teddy had eaten too many potatoes. Aunt Betty could only laugh picturing Teddy in the little vest that barely made it around his belly.

One of Dad's favorite potato dishes was potato salad. Toward the end of his life he asked me if there would be potato salad in heaven. I assured him there would be, and Dad said, "Then I'm ready to go." At our family get-togethers, we still serve potato salad in honor of my father. While he might not be present with us physically, he is there in spirit and so is his much-loved bowl of potato salad.

That's the kind of storytelling I heard from the time I was little. When I first began to write, I worked to re-create the same story-telling ethos I'd seen practiced by my father and his family.

Gifts from Our Guests: Fathers sometimes give the gift of demonstrating how to use our skills to chart out our paths.

Letters Tucked in a Diary

My dad was my encourager. It was as natural to him as breathing. Like me, he unfortunately never did well in school. I believe he was probably dyslexic. He had trouble with math too, yet as an upholsterer, he could figure out square yardage on a davenport just by looking at it. He had such an incredible eye. He was the one who encouraged me when I was struggling in school.

I'm not athletic. I love to swim, and I walk the local track, but I'm not the least bit athletic. In contrast to me, my father was very athletic. He and my mom danced from the time I can remember. It was such fun just to watch them. When they danced, everybody in the room turned to look. They never took classes, but on the dance floor they were naturals. People would talk about them because they were such an attractive, dynamic couple. They had friends wherever they went and were on many a guest list.

Dad was, in many ways, all the things I was not. And yet my father always seemed inordinately proud of me. His acceptance and approval helped me through the tough, ugly-duckling years of my youth.

After I left home, my dad wrote me letters, which I read and reread, tucking them into my diary. I still treasure those letters. I wonder if he knew how much his written words of encouragement meant to me.

As I've come to know my heavenly Father, I can see that my own father's unconditional acceptance of me laid the groundwork for my understanding and receiving God's love.

Gifts from Our Guests: The gift of a father's positive impact can usher us into a healthy relationship with God, the ultimate Father. In contrast, the unwanted gift of wounds and discord can lead us to hunger for and reach out for healing from the perfect father — our heavenly Father.

Seeking Father's Smile

Not everyone is as fortunate as I was to be blessed with such a wonderful, loving father. Some have a more complicated relationship. Issues of abandonment, alcoholism, abuse — all may figure into father stories, many of which I've heard from friends. We ask the question: Did God invite that kind of dysfunction into our lives?

I wish I had the answer to that, but I

don't. What I do know is that a troubled father/child relationship sometimes builds a resiliency that forms a basis for great achievement. History is full of stories of overcomers whose relationships with their fathers were painful. I can't help but wonder if these overcomers could have achieved their success had they not had the abrasion in that key paternal relationship.

It reminds me of the story the famous comedian Jerry Lewis told of his father, vaudeville performer Danny Lewis. All his life Jerry sought his father's approval. It didn't matter what he did; it was never enough for his father. His dad would always withhold his approval, saying, "You ain't got it yet, kid." He used to tell Jerry that it was Broadway that mattered, not television, not film, not even Jerry's command performance before Queen Elizabeth. For as long as he lived, Jerry's dad repeated the same phrase whenever his son sought his approval — "You ain't got it yet, kid." After twenty years Jerry Lewis finally agreed to do *Damn Yankees* on Broadway. He often told the story about how, coming off the stage after opening night, he felt his father saying, "*Now* you got it, kid." And Jerry finally sensed that hard-won approval.

There's no question that God calls fathers

to a high standard. If your father fell short of that standard, the challenge is to root out any bitterness. Bitterness will damage and taint lives. Instead, look at the positive results of your dad's influence, including the good results from his bad behavior, to balance the negative impact you suffered. That new twist on revisiting old wounds can have a profoundly positive impact.

The most healing act of all is forgiveness. It's not easy, but forgiveness can set you free.

> *Gifts from Our Guests:* Even if you can find no other positive life results from your father, discovering the power to forgive, and applying that power to your relationship with your father, could very well be the "gift" you received at having your father on God's guest list for your life.

A Bread Truck

Tom Krause, coach and motivational speaker, tells an unforgettable story[1] of his father.

The earliest memory I have of my father is one of me as a young boy holding his hand by his two last fingers as we walked together. His hands seemed so large that his fingers were all I could actually grip. He always took me with him to ball games even at my young age. I will never forget that.

As I grew older I remember dad and me listening to high school basketball games together on an old transistor radio. I would make a list of players' names on a piece of paper and keep track of how many points each would score as the game went on. Too small to stay awake for the whole game, I always fell asleep before the game ended. When I would wake up in the morning I would find the score sheet lying next to me. The score sheet would be filled out with the final score on it completed by my father before he carried me to bed.

My father was a bread deliveryman. I remember the times when my father would stop by the house in the early morning on those cold days when I was home from school over Christmas break. I used to ride on the floor of that bread truck as he delivered the bread to the stores. I don't know if those old trucks even had heaters but it didn't matter. The smell and warmth from the bread that had just come from the bakery ovens would make my mouth water and keep me warm both at the same time.

In high school I became very interested in athletics. My father would attend all my games. My junior year something special happened.

It was in algebra class during the spring of the year. Football season was long over. We had done well last season — qualifying for the playoffs for the first time in school history. I wanted us to do even better next year, my senior year. Then the idea hit me. I didn't wait till after school. During my lunch break, I drove over to a print shop and ordered business cards with a simple, direct prophesy —

"BOONVILLE PIRATES — 1974 STATE CHAMPIONS!"

When the cards were printed, my teammates and I distributed them all over town.

Teachers pinned them to classroom bulletin boards. Merchants taped them in store windows. Pretty soon those cards were everywhere. We worked hard at getting the cards all over town. There was no escaping them, and that's what we wanted. We wanted our goal to be right in front of us, for all to see, impossible to overlook, no matter where we went. Although we faced skepticism, it only served to strengthen our conviction to make our dream a reality. Our school had never won a state title in any sport — we were determined to change that history.

By the time football practice started in late August we were focused. There was a sense of urgency that made us a close team. From day one we gave more in practice, paid more attention to detail as we executed assignments sharply. With our goal imprinted in our minds and hearts — "BOONVILLE PIRATES — 1974 STATE CHAMPIONS!" we marched through the season undefeated and stepped into the playoffs with a sense of destiny.

The first playoff game matched us against a powerhouse team that was riding a twenty-eight-game winning streak. We knew we were in for a fight, but as the intensity of the game increased, so did our determination. We won, pulling away in the second half. That win brought us to the brink of our goal, a match-up with the defending state champions for the title.

We went into preparing for the big game with the same intensity and focus we had shown as a team all season. Then it started to snow. A huge winter storm blew through the area. School was canceled; roads were closed; transportation systems shut down. Still, somehow every member of the team made it to the school gym and we practiced for the biggest game of our lives in tennis shoes.

Our coach received a phone call before practice the day before the game telling us that state officials were thinking of canceling the game and declaring co-champions because of the severe weather. We were asked if we would accept such a decision. "No way" was our response. This was our year. We were not going to get this close and not take a shot at the title.

That night my father came to me and sadly announced that he would not be able to attend the game. He had to deliver the bread to the stores and the site of the game was over a three-hour drive from his route. He vowed to listen to every play on the transistor radio. Consumed with the anticipation of the game I acknowledged his comments without fully noticing his regret.

The next day as game time approached I couldn't help thinking about my dad.

As we arrived at the stadium we found the field buried in snow. The goalposts stuck out above a six- to eight-inch blanket of snow. Someone asked if snowshoes would be allowed as legal equipment. Undaunted we dressed for the game and began our warm-ups.

Frustration grew as both teams struggled to a scoreless first half. Slip, slide, fall down, dropped pass, missed blocks, fumbles were all either team had accomplished. There was a growing sense of urgency that time was running out on our dream.

In the locker room at half-time, Coach Reagan reminded us of all we had been through to get to this moment. Then he reached in his pocket and pulled out the card. Right there in front of us once again was our vision. "Do you want this?" he said. That is all he needed to say.

As I lined up for the second-half kickoff I happened to look up and noticed a blue and white bread truck pulling into the parking lot. Dad had delivered the bread and driven over three hours to see the second half of the game.

Playing conditions were as tough the second half as they were the first, but our determination won out over the playing conditions. We scored 34 points in the second half on the same field we couldn't score any on in the first half. Our year-long dream became reality. To this day I still have my card.

Years later I had become a teacher and coach. Early one morning I was awakened by the sound of the telephone ringing at 5:30 A.M. As I struggled to answer the phone I'll never forget the sound of the sheriff's voice on the other end telling me that my dad had just been killed in an automobile accident on his way to work. Cattle from a nearby farm had broken through a fence and wandered onto the highway. It was a dark, rainy morning, and my father never saw them as he came over a ridge. The impact spun the car sideways in the highway before a semi-trailer collided with it. He was killed instantly. As I listened to the story I could hear my heart beat in my ears. I hung up the phone devastated.

For a long time after that things really didn't matter to me. I went about my life but I really didn't care. It felt as if my heart had been torn away and in a sense it had. I went to work. I still taught school but I was just going through the motions.

One day I was on the school playground supervising a first-grade recess when a little boy walked up to me. As I looked down at him he reached up and grabbed my hand by my last two fingers — just like I used to do to my dad. In that moment my father came back to me. In that instant I realized that even though my father was gone — he had left me something behind. He had left me his smile. He had left me his compassion. He had left me his heart. When that little boy touched my hand I realized that all these wonderful gifts that I had loved so much about my father could be passed on to others. In that moment I understood the meaning of the word heritage.

I now spend my days passing on that heritage to my 8-year-old stepson and 3-year-old son; a heritage not only about fathers, sons and sports. A heritage filled with love.

Gifts from Our Guests: Sometimes the gift of love is given simply by our father's presence in our lives.

A Tin Box in the Attic

My dad was an upholsterer. He was one of the smartest businessmen I knew. He was also one of the poorest businessmen I knew.

Let me qualify that. Rather than calling him a poor businessman, I should say he grew up with a hearty distrust of banks. So anytime anyone paid him cash in the fifty years that he was an upholsterer, he put it in a tin box in the attic. He called it his retirement. As I think back now, he could have doubled, tripled, or even quadrupled his money if he'd put it in a bank with compounding interest, but as a child of the Depression, he simply didn't trust bankers, and so he kept the cash himself rather than investing it. I have since learned that many of the Depression generation did the same. If the place had burned down, he would've lost everything. So my father's retirement fund rested in a tin box in the attic.

But aside from a distrust of financial institutions, he had a natural business instinct. He understood customer service, but not in some formulaic way. He made his customers his friends, listening to them and meeting their needs. His work was flawless. He took great pride in the quality of each job. His goal was to exceed each customer's expectations. He made it a practice to give more than what was asked of him. If he promised a customer that a project would be done on a certain day, nothing would keep him from meeting that deadline. When he set the completion date, he worked in a cushion of time so that he could surprise them by having the job finished before the due date. And then he would take the extra fabric and make covers for the arms or the backs of the cushions. He gave added value long before the business community coined the phrase.

In all the years he ran his business, he rarely advertised. He didn't need to — it was all word of mouth, and in half a century of operating his shop, he never ran out of work. He was good at what he did, and those seeking quality flocked to my father's shop.

I don't have to look far to find my father's influence in my career. My publisher can attest to the fact that I'm like him when it comes to meeting my writing deadlines. I often refer to myself as a "value-added author." My goal is to give more than the publisher or reader expects. And, just like my father, who made his customers his friends, I've been blessed to be able to consider many of my readers my friends as well.

Gifts from Our Guests: The gift of a strong work ethic is a gift many fathers give by example.

TAKE NOTE

My father's letters are a tangible reminder of his influence in my life. My diaries are also filled with remembrances of my wonderful dad. Because our relationship with our heavenly Father is often affected by our relationship with our earthly fathers, the margins of my Bibles also tell some of what I've discovered about my God, my Father.

Here I have listed some ways I've dug deeper into my father's life and influence. You may want to do the same as you examine your own father's influence on you.

- Spending time, talking with him when he was alive
- Reading the letters he wrote me
- Listening to others tell stories of him
- Writing about him both in my journals and in my fiction. I believe my readers catch glimpses of my dad in many of my wise, encouraging characters.

RSVP

I'm not a father, so I'm not even going to attempt to give advice on how to be influential as a father, but let me tap into the wisdom of many wise fathers. Educational consultant James B. Stenson asked veteran fathers what advice they'd pass on to younger dads.[2] Here's some of the cautionary advice they offered:

- Don't neglect your wife. She needs what we all need: understanding, affection, gratitude, support, and appreciation. For sure, she doesn't get these from the kids when they're small. So if she doesn't get them from her husband either, then she doesn't get them at all.
- Don't underestimate your children. Have high ambitions for their swift, step-by-step growth into maturity. We all tend to become what we think about, and kids tend to become what their parents expect of them.
- Don't treat teenagers like large children. Think of them, and treat them, as near-adults. Pull them up, fine-tune their consciences, welcome them to adult reality. Show them how to balance a checkbook, pursue a job, work

professionally, please their bosses, deal respectfully with the opposite sex.

- Don't ever tell your teens that the high-school years are the best part of their lives. This isn't true. Adolescence is, in fact, one of life's toughest times: teens have to cope with blunders and glandular upheavals, surfing up and down learning curves.
- Don't let your children weasel out of commitments. Don't let them take back their word on a whim. Before they make promises or otherwise commit themselves to a course of action, press them to think consequences through and understand their terms, because you will hold them to their word.
- When you're correcting your children and they petulantly ask, "Why?" — don't argue with them. If they're looking for an explanation, give it once only. If they persist with "Why?" then they're looking for an argument, not an explanation.
- Don't let your kids dress in such a way as to bring shame to the family. Nobody has a right to do this.
- Don't miss small opportunities to talk with your kids. Listen politely and

respectfully. You can talk with them while driving, doing dishes and other chores together, walking and biking, working on hobbies you share, tucking them into bed.

- Don't shout at your kids so often. It's a waste of breath. If one of your children needs a talking-to, take him or her out for a walk or a soda — and say what you have to say in a calm, serious way. Don't forget to listen, too.

- Don't get trapped into blazing arguments, especially with your teens, and most especially if you have a temper. Words can wound and take a long time to heal. If tempers are flaring, put off the discussion till later — that evening or the next day — when you've both cooled down. If you go too far, be the first to apologize.

- Don't forget to praise your children, and be specific about it. Kids need a pat on the back from time to time. We all do. Give praise for effort, not just success.

- Come down to your children's level, but don't stay there. Kids are kids, and you have to come down to their level to take them by the hand. But your long-term goal is to bring them up to your own level — to lead them, patiently over time, to think and act like mature grown-ups. So live like a grown-up.

I will sing of the LORD's great love forever; with my mouth I will make your faithfulness known through all generations.

— PSALM 89:1

NINE:
FORBIDDEN STRAWBERRIES,
HEALING FOOD,
AND MOONLIT RACES
THE IMPORTANCE OF FAMILY

April 1, 1933. The Nazi *Sturmabteilung* (SA) stood shoulder to shoulder in front of Jewish shops across Germany in a one-day boycott that was the first measure Adolf Hitler mounted against the Jews. The Star of David had been painted on the doors along with signs that read, "Don't buy from Jews" and "The Jews are our disgrace."

Most Germans hurried by, pretending they hadn't intended to shop that day anyway. Who could have guessed that this was the first volley of what would become known as the Holocaust? But the threatening stance of the Brown Shirts and the fear etched on the faces of the shopkeepers kept everyone far, far away.

Everyone, that is, except for one small ninety-one-year-old grandmother. Oma Bonhoeffer may have been diminutive in stature, but she was fearless. She pushed her way through the surprised SA guards, walked into the cordoned-off shop, and selected her basket of strawberries. She took out her coin purse, paid for them, chatted for a moment with the shopkeeper, and then pushed past the guards one more time, heading back out onto the street toward home.

Who was this woman?

She was the grandmother of Dietrich Bonhoeffer, one of the few pastors in Germany who, early on, stood in opposition to the national church that supported Hitler. He became a leader in what was called the Confessing Church. Regardless of personal cost and danger, Bonhoeffer stood in courageous opposition to the Führer and his policies. As one Anglican bishop who had been his friend in England wrote of him, "He was crystal-clear in his convictions; and young as he was, and humble-minded as he was, he saw the truth and spoke it with complete absence of fear." Bonhoeffer would lose his life in an extermination camp just three weeks before American forces liberated that camp.

Many people will look at a hero like Dietrich Bonhoeffer and wonder how God raises up such men who fearlessly face down evil. There are many factors, of course, but if we were to look at the guest list for his life, one of those people on it would be his fearless ninety-one-year-old Oma.

Gifts from Our Guests: When we unravel the threads of who we are, we discover the gifts of our extended family tightly woven into the very warp and woof of our personalities.

A Bitter Root

My mother grew up in a very strict household. My grandfather was a Russian immigrant who came to this country as a young man. His wealthy family escaped the revolution but had to leave everything behind. He had grown up as a privileged son. He spoke six languages and was a noted musician, but the only work he could get in this country was as a coal miner and then later as a farmer. It made him an angry, bitter man.

My grandmother also came from Russia, but she was much younger when she arrived. When she met my grandfather, she was widowed with five young children and living with her parents. I believe her parents arranged their marriage. Florian needed a wife, and my great-grandparents wanted to see their daughter and her five children settled. This wasn't exactly a match made in heaven. They said, "We'll buy you a farm. Marry our daughter." So my grandfather married her, and they had eight children together. My grandfather, with all his education and skill, worked the farm, but he wasn't a farmer. From the stories my mother told me, the family nearly starved.

This was my mother's heritage. A bitter father and a mild mother who never spoke up for herself, who went along with whatever her parents or her husband decreed. My mother's childhood was too often harsh and joyless.

I don't remember Grandmother Zimmerman; she lived in North Dakota and died when I was four or five, and yet I see her influence in my life even today. For one thing, despite how mild and submissive she was with my grandfather, her disciplinary methods were strict and unbending. My mother decided that she would never discipline as she was disciplined, so I had a lenient upbringing. I struggled to find boundaries, so when my children came along, I tried to strike a happy medium. It's interesting how the pendulum swung a little too far in one direction and then a little too far in the other. I'd like to say I managed to balance it in the middle, but I guess we'll have to wait until my children or grandchildren write a book on parenting to see if I came anywhere close. Hindsight is 20/20, of course.

But Grandma Zimmerman showed love in the only language she knew. She cooked. And, oh my goodness, could she cook. She taught my mother everything she knew. And my mother, in turn, taught me. When Mom moved away from home and joined her older half sister in Washington State, her mother gave her a brown composition book — a journal — filled with household hints and recipes. Want to know how to make soap? It's in there. And she instructs how one can tell that beans are perfectly cooked. It's by the aroma, and my grandmother tries to describe that fragrance in words.

I definitely see the patterns here — a journal, recipes, cooking, using the written word to capture sensory things. They say the apple doesn't fall far from the tree. When we examine our families, we're likely to find the roots of who we are. When I think of my mother's family, I can see that the bitter root did not take hold. For that I'm thankful.

Food and Love

I have to laugh when I realize how important a theme food is in the story of my extended family. Food and love were always intertwined. Not only through Grandma Zimmerman, but through Grandma Adler as well. Their heritage includes appreciation of good food, translating into good nurturing and love. In my family, when a person is hurting, someone pushes a plate in front of him and says, "Here, eat something; you'll feel better."

I can see where I get my love of food and cooking. I still have my mother's recipes in the old cardboard box she had either in high school or as a young wife and mother. I also have the green tin box of recipes I had when I left home after high school. I wrote out each recipe card by hand.

Early in my career, for five years or so, I sent out small books of recipes I had collected and loved to share with my readers. In return, my readers shared their favorite recipes with me. In a fun way it makes sense that I'm now publishing my own cookbooks.

Gifts from Our Guests: The inheritance of the nurturing influences is a gift from family that can often be remembered through the aromas and flavors of food shared with family.

My father had a wonderful mother and a huge extended family. My childhood spilled over with family — a sibling, cousins, aunts, uncles . . . We all lived in the same neighborhood except for Aunt Betty, her younger brother, my uncle Jerome, and their families. We all attended the same church. We often went on family vacations together. Every weekend, it was family, family, and more family. I grew up watching my uncles playing pinochle and horseshoes, and the women talking food and cooking. And, oh, could they ever cook!

In the baby-boom years following World War II, there were five Adler offspring born within fourteen months of one another. We were spread across two grades. David and I were in one grade, and Terry, Doug, and Linda were in the grade below us. The five of us were more like brothers and sisters than cousins.

And it wasn't just us five. There were older cousins and younger cousins too. Big families. We looked up to older cousins, and the little ones looked up to us. I remember my younger cousin Cherie's being in awe of me because I wore nylon stockings with seams. She would stare at them and wistfully say that she only hoped that when she wore stockings she could get the seams as straight as mine. By the same token my older cousin Betty Ann influenced me, and I attended

St. Joseph Academy. She and my aunt Gerty had gone there.

My older cousins used to talk about our grandma Adler and how beautifully she could crochet. They said she could be in her rocking chair, rocking and snoring, and still never miss a stitch of her crochet. I believe I must have inherited my love of needlework from this grandmother I hardly remember.

Knitting has followed me all through my life. It was a lifeline when I struggled in school. I knit for my own children when they came along, and now I knit for my grandbabies. I also knit for charity. I even have Debbie Macomber knitting pattern books. Recently I signed a contract with Universal Yarn for my own yarn collection with my share of the proceeds going toward charity. It's pure fun for this knitting enthusiast. All those years ago, when I listened to my cousins tell needlework stories about Grandmother Adler — it was God's foreshadowing. I believe He gently led me in that direction.

Taking the time to reflect on my extended family has helped me discover more fully who I am and instills in me a sense of belonging, of tribe. That awareness then spills out in my determination to impart that same sense of belonging to my children, grandchildren, nieces and nephews, and so on.

Gifts from Our Guests: The gift of life direction is often received through the influence of family.

Moonlit Races

A writing friend, Marilynn Griffith, grew up in the same kind of loving extended family as I did. She wrote a poem about it. Just reading it makes me realize we were both sitting on porches, but a country apart, loving and being loved by family. Here's how she described those summer days in a blog post I clipped a few years back:

I'm scrambling to tie up a few loose ends so that I can cook up a little somethin' somethin' come Monday. I always get teary-eyed because growing up, my uncle Dave used to have a slamming fireworks celebration every year there in Springfield, Ohio. I'm talking slamming like he planned all year for it and I seldom see commercial light displays that compare. I had two aunts who lived a block away and there was an elementary school across the street (Lincoln.

You know every black neighborhood had a Lincoln school back in the day . . . and a Martin Luther King Jr. Road, of course). Folks would bring lawn chairs and everything. Uncle Dave would have stuff from Indiana, Kentucky, everywhere.

And food? Well, I didn't come by my — er, statuesque-ness for nothing. The folks in my family can cook. My aunt Charlene would make stuff I've never seen since, like rhubarb pie ("What is that pink celery stuff? It's pretty good."), and my aunt Barb (Dave's wife and my mother's sister) would have snap peas and white corn from her garden, fresh flowers from her backyard. Both of them have passed now, but every time I see a green tomato, I think of Uncle Dave snapping one off the vine and frying it in cornmeal for a sandwich with Miracle Whip. (It sounds nasty, but it was good, y'all!)

We'd catch lightning bugs and race from one end of the block to the next. ("One thousand one . . . one thousand two — Go!") Those were the days when time went slow and sweet. Like honey. All my cousins were the finest brothers in town (and the girls some fine sistahs) and everybody would come out to see. My grandmother was sure to be holding court at a picnic table, all while pulling my hair back into place. ("Come here a minute, girl. Somebody give me a brush . . .") Times when my cousins lined the lawn with afros shaped like halos and backs straight as the sky. Good times.

I wrote a poem 'bout it a few years ago. I cried a minute ago reading it again. It goes like this . . .

Girl Summers by Marilynn Griffith

We ran moonlit races
on the Fourth of July.
I ate fried green tomatoes
and rhubarb pie.

There was Blue Magic pressing oil
Pony beads and tin foil
Rake picks and sauna suits
Pressing combs and stolen fruit

We took caravan trips
In big Chevrolets
I heard eight-track tapes
And made macramé

Honey skin and Afro Sheen
Bread with pork chops in between
Porch stoops and fireflies
Wrinkled hands and golden eyes

We ran moonlit races
On the Fourth of July
I grew ten feet deep
And one mile high

Gifts from Our Guests: The gifts of family often go far beyond that of our DNA. At its best, family gives us our sense of belonging.

How does one capture the collective memories of family? In these days of job transfers and long-distance relationships, family memories like those I described and like Marilynn's Fourth of July gatherings are becoming rarer and rarer.

We need to be intentional about gathering family together, and then we have to chronicle those gatherings. Here are some innovative ways that might help to draw your families closer:

- Scrapbooking. This is a pictorial journal — a wonderful way to capture memories and share them.
- Websites. It's a modern way to create a bulletin board of sorts that everyone can access no matter how far away. New babies, recipes, family history — all can be combined, and all will help connect the family, especially if the site is interactive.
- Facebook. It's easy to follow family members on Facebook. They even have a family feature that helps you link to others on your family tree.
- Email circles. I've heard of sisters creating an email loop so they can keep in touch no matter how impossible

their schedules. It's a modern version of the round-robin letter.

RSVP

Sometimes it's easier to think back on our families and discover what kind of influence they had on us than to look forward and try to plan what kind of influence we will have on our extended families.

Too many of us avoid family gatherings, talking half-jokingly about dysfunctional families. In sharing my family memories, I've tried to be honest — to highlight the good as well as the bad. As you've read through some of my stories, I'm guessing it's easy enough to identify some elements of what a psychologist might call dysfunction. But that's reality. If you look back to the chapter on mothers, you'll notice that in the story of the much-revered Susanna Wesley, she and her clergyman husband separated for a time over a heated political argument. No one is perfect.

In the Bible, God says, "And let us not neglect our meeting together, as some people do, but encourage one another, especially now that the day of his return is drawing near" (Hebrews 10:25 NLT). The author of Hebrews is talking about the church, but it can be applied to our families as well. We need to gather together and encourage one another. And if we don't cultivate relationships with one another, how can we be of mutual influence?

It's not much of a guest list if the guests don't attend the party.

No one abuses his own body, does he? No, he feeds and pampers it. That's how Christ treats us, the church, since we are part of His body. And this is why a man leaves father and mother and cherishes his wife. No longer two, they become "one flesh." This is a huge mystery, and I don't pretend to understand it all. What is clearest to me is the way Christ treats the church. And this provides a good picture of how each husband is to treat his wife, loving himself in loving her, and how each wife is to honor her husband.
— EPHESIANS 5:29–33 (THE MESSAGE)

TEN:
THE FORTUNE COOKIE, THE ENGAGEMENT CANOE, AND NO REGRETS

FIRST LOVE AND FOREVER LOVE

George Bernard Shaw once said, "First love is only a little foolishness and a lot of curiosity."[1] I sometimes think God brings those first loves into our lives as a way of giving us confidence for our forever love.

From the time I entered an all-girls Catholic high school, there was one boy at the boys' school across the street who caught my eye. Tom Kloster. I liked him because he was an altar boy and came from a large Catholic family. He was the oldest. I knew if I was going to marry anyone, I would want to marry him. I admired Tom Kloster from afar. I even got up the nerve to ask him to the Sadie Hawkins dance. Not just once, but three times. He always found an excuse not to go with me. You know, Pudgy Debbie.

My friends used to tease me and said I had Kloster-phobia. We never did date, not even once. He eventually married and had four children. At the last class reunion, I joked with him, saying, "You know, I loved you from afar." You know what he said? He said, "You asked me to the Sadie Hawkins dance? What grade were you in? What's your name again?" Tom didn't have a clue who I was until our class reunion. We laughed. Now we send each other Christmas cards every year.

My first real boyfriend was named Larry Moser. Sometimes when I've spent a whole day signing books, I tease Wayne that instead of signing the name Macomber, with all those letters, I should have married Larry Moser. I'd be done a lot sooner.

I went out with Larry for about eighteen months. What I loved about Larry was that we would exchange notes, because he was at the boys' school and I was at the girls' school. He was a year ahead of me. When he graduated, he went into the Army. That was even better, because I wrote him stacks and stacks of letters. I finally realized that I didn't love Larry. What I really loved was writing him all those notes and letters.

Gifts from Our Guests: The gift of discovering what we really love is often bestowed through people we love.

No Regrets

When God invited me to look for the invitations to His guest list for my life, it didn't take long for me to recognize that my husband, Wayne, was one of those people God had sent into my life. I'm reminded of the invitations I've received that ask me to respond with "Regrets Only." And I cringe to think that I almost crossed Wayne off the guest list.

Wayne and I married when I was still a teenager. He was the breadwinner and decision maker. I was the stay-at-home mother to our four children, all born within five years. Wayne, who worked as a construction electrician, paid the bills, while I took care of the house and children.

My first exposure to the Bible came when Marilyn Kimmel, our neighbor in Seahurst, a suburb of Seattle, invited me to attend Bible Study Fellowship. It didn't take me long to realize my need for Jesus Christ. Spiritually hungry, I made my commitment to Him in May of 1973, and by the end of that summer Wayne also accepted Christ as his Lord and Savior.

Our life together was good; we were on solid ground with each other and with the Lord. In 1978, when I decided I wanted to write books, Wayne was the first one to encourage me. In fact, he was the one who went out and rented that first typewriter on the rent-to-own plan. He believed in me. He encouraged me, and when the rejections started coming in, it was Wayne who buoyed my spirits and comforted me with the assurance that one day my books would sell.

Then, miracle of miracles, I sold that first book in September of 1982. My advance of four thousand dollars carried us through a bleak winter of unemployment. Construction was almost at a standstill, and Wayne and I were both grateful I was able to contribute for the first time to our family's income. Soon afterward I sold a second book and then a third. We took our first real vacation in years. Wayne and I were thrilled at my literary success.

Within a couple of years my writing income was larger than the amount Wayne brought into our family. Within five years I was paying more in income tax than he was earning.

Fissures formed in our marriage. Soon those small cracks became a huge, bottomless crevasse, and we found ourselves in a constant battle of wills. I resented Wayne for making decisions without including me. He resented my making decisions on my own, especially in my career, without talking matters over with him first. We both made mistakes; we were both stubborn and determined to have our own way. Instead of a cohesive unit, we were continually at odds.

Then in 1988 it became apparent that we could no longer live together. Wayne moved out, and frankly I was glad to see him go. He traveled to another state and worked there. The release from the terrible tension in our household was instantaneous. The children and I were better off without Wayne, I decided.

I hired my attorney. Wayne hired his. I filed for the divorce first, although Wayne agreed the marriage was over.

It didn't take long for the honeymoon period of life without Wayne to end. The children were hurting emotionally and mentally. I was, too, although I was much too proud to admit it.

Then in church one Sunday a visiting pastor mentioned the benefits of praying every day for one hour. Seeing how badly the children hurt because of the pending divorce, I decided if there was ever a time in my life when our family needed prayer, it was then. As a result of that sermon, every morning I got down on my knees and prayed for a solid hour. I did this for weeks. I didn't ask God to heal the marriage (by this time the divorce was days from being finalized); instead, my prayers centered on the children and our life together. I prayed God would heal Wayne from the pain this divorce had caused him, and I asked God to bless my soon-to-be-ex-husband in a number of specific ways.

A week before the divorce was final and a full year after Wayne had moved out, he contacted me. He was still living and working in another state. Quite honestly I was surprised to hear his voice, as we had only communicated through our attorneys.

"I don't want to do this," Wayne announced.

"You don't want the divorce?" I couldn't believe I'd heard him correctly. Wayne was the one who'd moved out and moved on.

"Frankly, the divorce isn't working for me."

This wasn't an answer to my prayers. I had put the marriage behind me. We had tried so many times before, and all our efforts had failed. I didn't believe another attempt to live together would change anything.

In the end, we compromised. Wayne moved back to the area and rented an apartment. Then we dated for six months before we made the decision for him to return to the family home. When he did move back in with the children and me, my husband stated that this new commitment had to be forever; otherwise the threat of divorce could become a revolving door. I saw the wisdom of his words. This year Wayne and I will celebrate our forty-second wedding anniversary.

God took the mess we had made of our marriage — He took the pain, the resentment, and the anger. Next, He sent us both our separate ways while He worked on our hearts. God worked on all the negative emotions, and through prayer, forgiveness, and an abundance of love, He gave us back a solid, loving marriage. I'm glad I didn't respond to God's invitation with "regrets."

Gifts from Our Guests: The gift of weathering the seasons of life together is only experienced when we do not give up in the dry seasons.

The Engagement Canoe

My friend shared with me a story told by Pastor Gary Cole.[2] It speaks beautifully to the richness that comes from shared love and shared interests. Here's Pastor Cole's story:

When Luther Anderson, a budding accountant, proposed to Ethel, a young schoolteacher, he vowed to give her a beautiful diamond engagement ring. "If it's all the same with you, I'd rather have a canoe," replied Ethel. This signified the beginning of a match made in heaven. The Andersons were married for over fifty years. They used the engagement canoe for their honeymoon in the Boundary Waters area of Minnesota. Luther wrote several books on outdoorsmanship — canoeing, fishing, and hunting — in the Upper Peninsula of Michigan, northern Wisconsin, and Minnesota.

Luther died in 1982, the year before I moved to Ironwood. Ethel shared the story about her engagement canoe one afternoon while she and I were paddling in the canoe out on Spider Lake. The canoe was still in perfect condition. It was too large for her to get into the water by herself, since she was eighty years old. She liked to invite people down to the log cabin that she and Luther built on the shore of Spider Lake in the early years of their marriage. They felled, trimmed, and notched all the trees they used to build the cabin. Later they constructed a beautiful cottage next door. Visitors and guests always had the privilege of canoeing with Ethel. She said she felt closest to Luther when she was paddling in her engagement canoe.

I have often wondered what happened to the canoe when Ethel died a few years ago. If she had had her druthers, I expect she would have been buried in it.

Gifts from Our Guests: The gift of a partner who shares the very things we love increases our joy.

A Fortune Cookie

I understand now that when I singled out Tom Kloster for my attention, I had focused on what I admired in a man more than on Tom himself. Someone from a big, happy family, someone spiritual who was close to God, somebody who wanted children and the same things I wanted. It's funny that the man I married was my complete opposite. Wayne did not come from a big family. It was just basically Wayne and his mother living with his grandparents. Nor did he have that large extended family I had. Family wasn't that important to Wayne. We are so completely different, and yet God brought us together. God meant Wayne for me.

I may have started my writing career as a romance writer, but forget romantic — Wayne married me on the advice of a fortune cookie. We were engaged to be married. I had my engagement ring. My mom and dad had bought my wedding dress, had put the money down on the hall for the reception, and had booked the date with the church. Wayne was working for an engineering company but decided he wanted to become an electrician. It meant a thirty-dollar-per-week cut in pay. Back in 1968 thirty dollars a week represented a lot of money — about a third of his weekly income. Wayne didn't know if he could make it financially given this huge pay cut.

Because of his changing financial situation, he felt we should delay the wedding for a year. When he told me, I said, "I definitely want to support you in any way I can, Wayne, but my parents have already committed a lot of money to this wedding. If you feel we must do this, I'll let you tell them." Wayne agreed he would.

My mother and father had come to Seattle for a meeting, and we all went to dinner together at a Chinese restaurant. I told them that Wayne had something he wanted to tell them.

My stomach churned throughout the meal as I waited for Wayne to broach the subject of delaying the wedding for a year. When was he going to tell them? After we finished eating, my father passed the fortune cookies around. When Wayne opened his fortune cookie, it read, "What's a job compared to a good marriage?" I could see him fingering that little strip of paper.

I said, "Do you want to tell my parents something, Wayne?"

He looked down at his fortune and then said, "Yes, I want to thank you for everything you've done for us. Debbie and I are going to get married."

He carried that fortune with him for many years in his billfold. He may still have it. Yes, my husband married me on the sound advice of a fortune cookie.

That was Wayne. He is the very opposite of me, and yet, if you were to ask Wayne why God brought him into my life, he would be the first to tell you, "God brought me into Debbie's life to be her support, to be her encourager, to be her balance." If it were not for Wayne, we wouldn't live part of the year in Florida, where our lifestyle is so completely different from that in Washington State. He longed for the year-round sunny climate, opening us up to an entirely different life. We are much more relaxed and social in Florida than in Washington.

One of the reasons I fell in love with Wayne was because he loved to read. For years after we were first married, on New Year's Eve we'd build a fire in the fireplace and stay up all night and each read a book. That was the most incredible evening to us, to have that peace to sit up all night and simply read.

Wayne brings balance to me. I'm a driven, compulsive worker. He makes me look at things in a different way. I picked up one of my old journals and read where I was thanking the Lord for the husband that He had sent into my life. Wayne lets me be who I am. He takes pride in me.

That's one of the reasons I share with him the guest-book entries that readers leave on my website. After I've read and answered them, I have my office email him the ones that praise my stories, because he's directly responsible for my being published. I want him to understand how his encouragement of my writing has helped someone else.

Gifts from Our Guests: The gift of our polar opposite can fill in our blanks, challenge us to stretch, and complete us. The gift of shared interests can draw us together. Having both gifts wrapped up in the same person is a delightful gift to open!

Marriages take work. If you are married, you probably already know that this relationship at times may warm us, stretch us, make us grow, affirm us, and sometimes totally exasperate us. Borrowing from Socrates, we could say that the unexamined marriage is not worth living. If we want to avoid circling around and around and making the same mistakes over and over, we need to learn from each mistake and each victory. I believe that when and if God brings two people together, He uses marriage to refine and shape them to be more like Jesus.

I've often used my year-end goal-setting time to take stock of my marriage. You might want to formulate a set of questions to do the same for your marriage. Here are mine:

- Am I helping Wayne reach his goals?
- What one word describes our relationship right now?
- Are we communicating honestly and openly?
- Am I listening to Wayne?
- What one thing do I wish I could do better as a wife?
- Are we spending enough time together?

- Do we talk about us and not just the children or other people?
- Do we have fun together?

Working out honest answers to these questions each year gives us a way to chart our progress from year to year. Intentionally seeking to grow the relationship provides insurance against falling into a rut.

Amy Bloom said, "Love at first sight is easy to understand; it's when two people have been looking at each other for a lifetime that it becomes a miracle."[3]

RSVP

As we talk about the influence of our "forever love" in our lives, we need to always remember that we were called into that person's life as well. While we're examining the marriage itself, it doesn't hurt at all for us to do some self-evaluation about our own influence on our spouses.

- Am I kind? It sounds simple, but if kindness is practiced, it could revitalize families.
- Am I an active listener? Do I show that I care about what's being said?
- Do I do the little things, the caring things, instead of worrying about the grand gestures or big gifts?
- Do I treat my spouse with as much deference in private as I do in public?
- Do I forgive and seek restoration?
- Do I say things to honor my spouse in the way I speak about him or her?

When we build our spouses up rather than tear them down, we'll be modeling the way the Lord treats us.

It has given me great joy to find some of your children walking in the truth, just as the Father commanded us.

— 2 JOHN 1:4

ELEVEN:
HUMBLE PIE, SURPRISE BABIES, AND BROKEN WINGS
OUR CHILDREN

When each of my babies came into the world, I marveled at the miracle entrusted to me. When children are newborn and helpless, all we see are the possibilities. Sometimes we are awed by the responsibility, and other times we are filled with hopes, dreams, and plans. As each one of my four children joined our family, I had no doubt each was sent from God. No mistakes there. Put them on my guest list immediately — they will honor Wayne and me. They will do us proud.

Well . . .

We're talking honest here, right?

I still believe my children were sent from God, and they have changed me in ways I never anticipated. But let's face it, those helpless compliant little infants are only with us for a short time. All too soon they assert themselves. Often right out of the birth canal. I'm thinking God gives us children to keep us humble.

Four children — four strong personalities. I'm thankful that my now-grown kids are committed to living their lives honestly, warts and all, because too many parenting books present a sanitized version of family life. We read them and feel guilt-stricken, thinking, *What perfect children. What did I do wrong?* I'm here to tell you I do not have perfect children. Of course, they did not have perfect parents either. Not even close!

The Bible verse for this chapter is 2 John 1:4: "It has given me great joy to find some of your children walking in the truth, just as the Father commanded us." That is our goal, to have our children walking in the truth. My four believe in keepin' it real, so in this chapter I'm going to tell you about some of my children and grandchildren and how having them on my guest list has changed me. Let me assure you, they have given me permission to do so, and for their willingness and their vulnerability, I respect them immensely.

Called by Name

I have always loved the verses, " 'Fear not, for I have redeemed you; I have summoned you by name; you are mine. When you pass through the waters, I will be with you; and when you pass through the rivers, they will not sweep over you. When you walk through fire, you will not be burned; the flames will not set you ablaze. For I am the LORD your God, the Holy One of Israel, your Savior' " (Isaiah 43:1–3). *Called by name* — that's a powerful concept.

Names are important. I took a long time naming my children, but as my daughters grew up, I wondered if I had their names switched. What kind of mother looks at her newborn and gives her a name opposite of who she is? Jody Rose is named after my mother, Rose. And Jenny — my Jenny Adele — is named after Wayne's mom, Marie Adele. But as Jenny grew up, with her thick dark hair and brown eyes, I could see that she resembled my side of the family far more than Wayne's. She is so much like me and the rest of the Adlers. And Jody looked so much like Wayne's mother, Marie. One time his mother sent me a newspaper clipping of her from the forties. I opened it and thought, *What is Jody doing in the newspaper?* But it wasn't Jody; it was Marie. Jody has the Scott nose. She has Wayne's eyes. The shape of her face . . . I mean she is all Macomber.

My goodness, I gave those girls the wrong names, I thought.

And it was not only looks. For years Jody did not get along with my mother — two strong personalities, neither of whom ever hesitated to speak her mind.

But in those last months of my mother's life while I was living on both coasts, flying back to Washington from Florida every two weeks to check on Mom, it was Jody who looked after my mother. She was the one who took Mom to the doctor when I couldn't be there. It was Jody who came to visit her in the memory-care facility every single day. And Jody was the one who held Mom's hand with me as Mom passed from life into death.

So I guess I didn't give Jody the wrong name after all. God knew from the beginning, and through those turbulent teen years, how close Mom and Jody would grow toward the end of Mom's life.

When Wayne's mother died this year, Jenny changed her first name to Adele so she could have her grandmother's name. Yes, God knew.

Gifts from Our Guests: The gift of God's comfort comes in realizing that God knows, and loves, our children even better than we do.

Surprise Babies

In the 1970s advice columnist Ann Landers asked the question "If you had it to do all over again, would you have children?"[1] Ten thousand readers responded, and a full 70 percent said no. The reasons varied, ranging from neglect by grown children to disappointment, but the results staggered the nation. At the time, I was horrified by the results. I looked at my four little ones playing on the floor and couldn't imagine wishing them away. Well, most days.

Now that my children are grown, I can understand a little better. I'm guessing it wasn't that the parents didn't love their children but quite the opposite. They never expected that they would love so fiercely that it hurt.

When my older daughter, Jody, told us she was pregnant — unmarried, young, and pregnant by a man she met during a time of rebellion — we suffered a pain that was almost physical. Our beautiful daughter — so young, a product of a Christian school and home, and yet so very rebellious — was pregnant. I'll admit it. I felt ashamed. What would the people at church think? What would my family think? My grandchild — a baby born out of wedlock. I guess that term isn't used anymore.

I struggled. Let me tell you, during those months of waiting, I spent time on my knees, asking God to search my heart to root out any bitterness that might be skulking around. After praying, we told her we would support her and help her to keep her baby. I wasn't actively looking for those people God promised to send into my life back then, but if I had been, this little one would have been at the top of my list.

I was present in the delivery room when Jazmine was born. She was born by cesarean section, so they took her away immediately to clean and weigh her. A nurse asked if I wanted to follow them into the nursery. Without hesitation I said yes. As I walked into the nursery, that tiny, beautiful baby turned her head and looked straight at me. No, it was like she looked *into* me. The most amazing thing happened when her eyes connected with my eyes. My heart began to pound, and a physical sensation went straight through me.

I tell this story to Jazmine every year on her birthday, and as I've tried to explain it, it was almost as if talons planted themselves deep into my heart. All my misgivings fell away, and I knew I was going to love this baby. Unreservedly. I cannot imagine what my life would have been like had Jazmine not come into it.

Gifts from Our Guests: The gift of being challenged and profoundly changed is a gift we often resist with every fiber of being, especially when the gift is given through our children. But it is a gift of great worth beyond measure.

Broken Wings

My first son, Ted, has been a rock. Not that he hasn't had trouble that has caused his dad and me to spend many a sleepless night, but it usually wasn't of Ted's making. He's a wonderful father. Each one of my children is an amazing parent — loving and nurturing. But Ted has such a heart for people — he loved and cared for my father and even gave the eulogy at Dad's funeral. That's Ted.

Dale, our youngest, is the one who kept me praying. As I was recuperating from recent knee-replacement surgery, Dale suggested he should get credit for my new bionic knee because of all the time I spent on my knees in prayer for him.

Dale was a challenge, and yet he is such a blessing and incredible joy in my life. You cannot be around Dale and not laugh and have a good time. He's simply a fun, fun person. He's the life of our family. When he comes into the room, he is the center of attention because he's so full of life.

Like my father and me, Dale is a natural-born storyteller. As a little boy, he would find rocks and bring them home and say, "Mom, this rock is worth twelve million-zillion dollars." And he would have this complicated story about the rock and why it was worth so much. By the time he was done spinning his tale, you'd look at the rock and halfway believe him. This penchant for storytelling is a gift in many ways, but it comes with a flip side. Dale is also a gifted schmoozer. He can make up stories that are so believable, you want to believe him. We usually do.

Dale is also an alcoholic. It was a long time before Wayne and I recognized his problem, and by then it had almost ruined his life. Dale likes to please people — to tell them things that will make them happy. He doesn't like to share the ugly stuff, but then who does? Too often things would get to the point of desperation before he'd come to us for help.

He's been sober for three years now, at this writing, but it doesn't change the fact that he has the personality traits of an addict. He has to constantly fight it. Dale reminds me of the opening words of *A Tale of Two Cities* — "It was the best of times, it was the worst of times."

Dale and his wife, Laurie, wanted children more than anything, but it just wasn't happening. They tried in vitro fertilization, but five attempts failed. It was during this time that Dale unraveled. He left his wife, had an extramarital affair, and found that he was to become a father. It was enough to snap him out of the downward spiral he was on. Talk about a surprise baby.

As Dale embraced sobriety, he and Laurie began to work on their marriage and eventually reconciled. They both fell in love with the little baby and have been working with the baby's mother on a joint-custody plan to parent him. It's not the path Wayne and I would have chosen for our children or for our grandchild, but it's reality. And this little child is precious and dearly, dearly loved by our family and by Laurie's family too. As my friend said to me, "Do you think any of this took God by surprise?"

And it's not the final chapter by any means. This last summer Dale called me, clearly upset, and asked if he could come talk to his father and me. Generally when we receive phone calls like this, we figure Dale is at the end of his rope. Aware of the toll infertility and infidelity had taken on

Dale and Laurie's marriage, I asked him, "Honey, tell me what's wrong."

In response, my thirty-four-year-old son burst into tears and cried. "Mom, Mom, Laurie's pregnant."

Naturally I burst into tears as well. The dog began barking, and Wayne stood over me, demanding to know what had happened now.

Those were tears of joy, of unexpected happiness, of triumph for the positive changes Dale has made in his life. How blessed we are to have such a wonderful daughter-in-law as Laurie who has faithfully stood at Dale's side through all this and continues to love and support him. Baby Jaxon Paul Macomber was born March 10, 2010.

Wayne and I know Dale has a lifelong challenge ahead of him. When Dale told me about Jaxon, I said, "You know, Dale, God was waiting for you to get your life straightened out. You had to get sober before He could bring a child with Laurie into your life."

You might wonder why I'd tell his story here — with permission of course. We've learned that when we live our lives with nothing to hide, it strips evil of any hold over us. If we always appear as if we have everything together, how are we ever going to be there for other hurting people? Dale believes that, and so do I.

Our life with Dale has been a rollercoaster ride. The highs have been exhilarating, and the lows have been devastating. God is not finished with Dale yet, just as He's not finished with any of us.

Four children and nine grandchildren — God knew. One thing I know — God has invited each of them into my life, and He has invited me into each of theirs. I can't wait to see what happens.

When children come into our families, we are usually good at taking photos, making scrapbooks, even filling in the blanks of the baby book, but I'd like to challenge us to do more.

We need to enrich our children with the prayers we prayed for them and the hopes we have for them. We need to pour out our hearts to them, to leave them a legacy of honesty when we're gone.

Here are some ideas:

- If you use more than one Bible, choose one for each child. As you read the Bible and write notes in the margin, think specifically of that child. It's a natural way to pass on a piece of yourself and a spiritual legacy.
- Even if you live close by, you can begin to write letters to your children. You don't even have to send them now. Tie them with a ribbon for them to read "someday." When we are gone, our children will treasure any little word from us much more than now, in the middle of our crazy-busy lives.
- If you like scrapbooking and making photo albums, try to leave room for

meaningful reflections about your child, your grandchild, or an event.

RSVP

I encourage you to be honest about your children. Look at the downs as well as the ups in light of what God's intention was in bringing them into your life. Then I challenge you to do the same regarding yourself as someone's parent or parent-in-law, daughter or son, daughter-in-law or son-in-law.

We didn't have much choice accepting the RSVP to be on the guest list of our family members, but why do you think God put you in that family? What do you bring to your parents, grandparents, children, grandchildren, and extended family?

As I watched my own wonderful children at times turn away from our teaching and head off in their own directions, I learned a lot about my relationship with God, my heavenly parent. I, too, have knowingly and willfully headed down a path that I knew took me away from my heavenly Father. Recognizing that fact motivates me to draw closer to God, to value, respect, and honor the parent-child bond that God invites me to enjoy.

How about you?

A friend loveth at all times.
— PROVERBS 17:17 (KJV)

Twelve:
A Broken Doll,
a Broken Childhood,
and a Friend Forever

CHILDHOOD FRIENDS

Her mother was almost frantic with worry when the first-grader came home from school a half hour late. "Where have you been?" she asked as soon as her daughter walked into the house.

"I'm sorry, Mommy." Tears smudged her cheeks. "Susan brought her glass doll to school today for show-and-tell. On the way home she dropped it, and the face got all broke."

The mother gathered her little girl into her arms. "So you stopped to help her fix the doll?"

"Oh, no," she said, shaking her head. "I don't know how to help her fix it. I just stopped to help her cry."

That's the best thing about our childhood friends. They stopped to help us cry. They also walked with us through the sometimes confusing maze of growing up. Aside from our families, some of the first people God invites into our lives are our childhood friends. Comedian and sage Bill Cosby once said, "The essence of childhood, of course, is play, which my friends and I did endlessly on streets that we reluctantly shared with traffic."[1] He's right. We played together. Sometimes I think that is what is missing from our adult friendships today. When we've played with friends, cried together and shared dreams, a bond is formed that is not easily broken.

The Urlachers were a family who lived about two streets over when I was growing up. We lived on Eighth, and they lived on Tenth. There were twelve kids in that family. My mom worked outside the home, so instead of going home to an empty house, I'd go over to the Urlachers'. I couldn't wait to go to their house. Their mom was always in the kitchen cooking, and the kids — well, I just loved being around all those kids. Sometimes even now I'll catch the smell of something simmering in the kitchen or a feeling of warmth as I open the door to the house and my mind goes back to those days. They even let me burp the baby and change its diaper. Can you imagine? The Urlachers had the gift of being able to make a lonely, misfit girl feel like part of a big, rambunc-

tious family. I'm still in contact with some
of the Urlacher children today.

A Friend Forever

I read somewhere that the reason our childhood friends are so important is that they
helped define us. Children tend to be more
open than adults. The friends we knew
when we were little often knew more about
us than friends of later years do — after we
learned to hide parts of our personalities
and became adept at fending off true inti-
macy. I still love watching a child approach
another child. "Will you be my friend?"
They haven't yet learned to protect themselves from potential rejection.

In fourth grade, I had my first Best Friend.
I didn't have many friends in the primary
grades. In first grade — because I was the
youngest and because I started school ten
days late — I got off to a slow start. Everyone had their friends, and I always seemed
to be lagging behind somehow. From that
first moment of stepping into the boys'
bathroom, I seemed destined to inadver-
tently humiliate myself. That continued during second and third grade, as well. I was so
far behind. I couldn't read. I was the only
girl in the lowest reading group. I was the
chubby, slow girl. Three long years.

The miracle happened the next year. Her name was Carol Brulotte. She came from the wealthiest family in our community. Her father had been a farmer but was killed in an accident. I remember something about a railroad crossing, a lawsuit, and a big settlement. Carol's mother sold the farm and moved into town. The Brulottes had a huge house. I shared a bedroom with my brother until I started junior high, so when I first visited and discovered that Carol and her three sisters each had her own bedroom — well, I hardly had words to even describe that kind of wealth. And not only did they practically live in a mansion, but they had servants — a housekeeper and cook! All the girls in school wanted to be Carol's friend because she was rich.

But Carol chose me to be her best friend. I don't know why — maybe because she and I both loved books and telling stories. Carol and her sisters used to have sleepovers on the weekends. Carol could invite only one friend, and her mother made her choose a different friend each week, not the same friend over and over. If Carol chose someone else, she'd always send me a note or whisper to me that I was really her best friend. In our class pictures, you'll always find me standing next to Carol.

Carol would go on real vacations every year — like to the Southern Hemisphere or Europe. I saved the postcards that she sent me in the fifth and sixth grades from Australia and New Zealand. I still have them.

After eighth grade Carol went on to boarding school, and I attended the local Catholic girls' high school. We kept in touch, but our lives went in different directions. I discovered new friends and so did Carol. If friends help define us, Carol's friendship gave me stature at a time when I felt beaten down. The best thing? We reconnected as adults and remain friends to this day.

Gifts from Our Guests: The gifts our childhood friends gave us can often only be seen in hindsight — the gift of seeing ourselves as valuable, and wanted; the gift of defining who we are.

A Broken Childhood

A friend of mine wrote a young-adult biography of a childhood Holocaust survivor, Anita Dittman. As Wendy began planning the book, she figured she would start Anita's story with the happy normal childhood before the trouble began. She'd then tell the story of the escalating hatred leading to Anita's capture and time in the work camp. She would tell the story about how, after liberation, Anita found her mother alive in the concentration camp and about their final immigration to America. Most of all she wanted to focus on one of Anita's childhood friends — one that was with her before her life fell apart and again when they reconnected. Wendy saw it as a thread that would tie the story together — a thread to illustrate how life continues.

With this rough plan in mind, she began the interviews with the now-octogenarian Anita. Wendy says that as Anita would begin building the story of one of these sweet childhood friends or young boyfriends, Wendy would always ask Anita, "So what happened to him?" or "What happened to her?"

It was always the same answer. Anita would get very quiet and say, "I don't know." If Wendy pressed, asking if she ever tried to track any of them down, Anita would just patiently explain that it wasn't like that. Records were gone. People who lived were scattered to the winds. People who didn't, well . . .

In the end Wendy abandoned her plan of tying the biography up in a neat circular redemptive story. In real life sometimes things don't get tied up. Sometimes we don't get all the answers we seek.

Gifts from Our Guests: The gift of lifetime friends is a gift we easily recognize and celebrate, but the gift of a friend who was on the guest list for only a brief visit is often a gift for a very special reason.

A Fresh Start

Even after I had made friends with Carol Brulotte in fourth grade, school was torture all the way through eighth grade. I'd been pigeonholed — slow, dumb, and incapable of doing the harder work.

In high school I went off to a girls' school, St. Joseph Academy. To me, it was a fresh start. I was escaping from everything that had been grade school.

The summer before high school I made a decision. I was tired of being miserable. I would be starting a new school, across town. I would begin fresh with people who were unaware of my struggles. I wouldn't have any of my cousins at this school. I decided to reinvent myself. I'd be popular and I'd be smart. If there was any way I could humanly accomplish it, I would make it happen. I would make a name for myself in a positive way.

When school started, I sat in the front seat of every class I was in. I raised my hand. I paid attention. I did my homework. I asked for extra-credit assignments. I was determined I was going to be smart.

Well, I wasn't.

I never once made the honor roll, but I compensated. I supported the school, attending every extracurricular event I could fit in. I put myself out there. I sold more chocolate bars than anybody else, painted more signs, and was determined to be positive about life. It was a change and a challenge. I was determined to do or die.

Part of that extracurricular commitment meant that I attended church every day. My dad dropped me off early. There was only one other person who was at Mass every day — Jane Berghoff.

I didn't know it at the time, but Jane had already decided to dedicate her life to God. She had decided to become a nun. We met each morning at church, and we became the very best of friends.

Jane entered the novitiate after high school and became a nun, though she never professed her final vows. An interesting thing happened. Her father was a nominal Catholic. The rest of the family was devout, but Jane's father didn't attend Mass. They had eight children. Jane was number five. Her father's sister was a nun, and even though he wasn't a devout Catholic, it would have meant the world to him if one of his daughters entered the convent. Jane, who was especially close to her father, decided early on in high school that she would be that one.

When she was in the convent, her father got sick and eventually died, but the convent would not allow her to go home to attend his funeral. They allowed no space in which she could grieve. Jane bottled her grief and dealt with this pain as best she could. It wasn't long until she developed hiccups. Yes, hiccups.

Those debilitating hiccups continued for three weeks. The sisters finally put her in the hospital. The doctors poked and probed. The psychologist believed it to be a medical problem, and the medical doctor said it was a psychological problem. Since they couldn't solve it, they sent her back to the convent, and the convent sent her home. Once she was home with her family, the hiccupping stopped.

Since her father had died, I believe Jane realized she did not have to fulfill her father's destiny for her. So she went on to nursing school and eventually married and had two daughters. We had met my first year in high school, at a time when I needed to reinvent myself. And a few years later Jane discovered she needed to do the same thing.

Jane and I are still the very best of friends. She has blessed me in untold ways. She has been a friend for all seasons.

Gifts from Our Guests: Our childhood friends gave us the gift of becoming more than we could have been without their influence.

TAKE NOTE

As we grow up, we tend to move on and move away from childhood friendships. Sometimes it's geographical; sometimes we outgrow friends; and sometimes friends just move in two different directions.

As you study God's guest list for your life, you'll learn important things about yourself and about those God sent into your life by writing about your childhood friends.

It's easier than ever with the Internet these days to find people with whom we've lost touch. As you continue to remember, you might want to look up some of your special childhood friends, if only to drop them notes and tell them what their friendships meant to you.

RSVP

Since we left childhood a long time ago, we can no longer answer God's RSVP to become a childhood friend to someone. But we can offer that friendship to a child in our lives like Mrs. Urlacher offered me. With twelve children in her house she certainly didn't need me coming over every day, but I felt welcome and a part of that family.

What a gift.

My friend Gail remembers an Englishwoman, Miss Lowe, who lived on her block in San Francisco. As a six- or seven-year-old, Gail would knock on her door and be invited in for a tiny cup of tea and a visit. Those visits were magical. Miss Lowe would show Gail some of her treasures — a glass snuff bottle painted on the inside, a tiny cloisonné pot, a window full of African violets. Every once in a while Miss Lowe would gift my friend with some tiny treasure. Gail grew up to become a designer of lovely intricate things. She credits Miss Lowe with helping whet her appetite for beautiful works of art.

When we take the time to befriend a little one, it keeps us in touch with the child inside us as well. I love what Madeleine L'Engle said in her book *Walking on Water:*

"I need not belabor the point that to retain our childlike openness does not mean to be childish. Only the most mature of us are able to be childlike. And to be able to be childlike involves memory; we must never forget any part of ourselves. As of this writing I am sixty-one years old in chronology. But I am not an isolated, chronological numerical statistic. I am sixty-one, and I am also four, and twelve, and fifteen, and twenty-three, and thirty-one, and forty-five, and . . . and . . . and . . ."

As iron sharpens iron, so one man sharpens another.

— PROVERBS 27:17

THIRTEEN:
A BRAINTHROB,
A BANKER, AND BUILDERS
OF TEAMS AND DREAMS
COLLEAGUES AND BUSINESS ASSOCIATES

Dale Dauten, author of the book *Better Than Perfect: How Gifted Bosses and Great Employees Can Lift the Performance of Those Around Them,* asked Mike Roemer, the chief operating officer of Blockbuster, to consider the best colleague he'd ever had — the one person he'd choose to work with again, if he could pick just one.

Here's how Dale tells it:

Mike Roemer immediately told me about a young star of the company, Shane Evangelist, saying, "He reeks of leadership. He energizes a room." So much so that at age 30, he was put in charge of Blockbuster Online.

I spoke with Shane and asked him how he energizes a room. He laughed and said he didn't know. As we talked, though, I soon spotted a "brainthrob" at work. He's the star of the Blockbuster organization because he invites those he works with to be stars.

For example, he concluded that the key to making Blockbuster Online profitable was to take a customer's order and get the DVD in an envelope and shipped out in less than 60 seconds. He explained that realization to his team and then said, "I'm wondering if there's some way to get the transaction down to, say, 50 seconds?" That's a brainthrob question. He didn't tell his team what or how; he offered a challenge. And they came back, smiling, and said, "We can do it in 40 seconds."

As for a tiny example of "lovably unreasonable," Shane found that on a flight with a junior employee. Because he travels frequently, Shane was upgraded to first class. During the flight, he moved to the back, sat next to the young colleague, and spent the entire flight discussing the rookie's future.

Is that a reasonable use of an executive's time? Only in retrospect, when we learn that before every meeting, Shane thinks through who will be in attendance and how he can honor or help each person there. So, the information gained back in the coach section of the airplane comes into play and gives Shane one view from his "organizational third eye."

When I interviewed people at all levels about their best-ever colleagues, what I heard were stories about the best in human nature, stories that happened to be set in the workplace.

These are the skills of tapping into the best of being human. There are some people who do their jobs *perfectly;* there are a special few who do them even *better.*

Healing in the Office

In the chapter on prickly people I talked about my three failed office assistants. After that experience I was more than gun-shy. But talk about God bringing someone into your life!

All I knew was I needed an assistant, and I needed somebody who would answer the phone and run a professional office — someone who would represent me well. I called an employment agency, and they sent Renate. The day she came in for the interview, she wore an exquisite hand-knit sweater. Being a knitter, I immediately picked up on that. My first thought was, if I run into a knitting problem, this is an accomplished knitter. I could get help. That's how inept I was in those early days. The scariest thing is that I hired her and almost fired her the first week. I was so careful in every aspect of this relationship. Renate had worked for another company for eighteen years before they downsized, moving her department to another state. She had been a workshop manager, developing seminars. She offered complex organization skills. Even at that, I was jumpy. I came out of my office several months later there and found her making a chart for her son's tasks at home. I asked her what she was doing and if I was paying for that time or if it was on her own time. She seemed embarrassed and then went out to lunch and for a walk.

Renate came back from her walk, apologized, and said it would never happen again. I kept her. And I thank God, because she was definitely sent to be on my guest list. She has grown with me, becoming vital to the success of my career. I gave her a second chance, and, to her credit, Renate took hold of it and became not only my right-hand person but my left hand and both feet as well.

Being a people pleaser, when I'm asked by someone to do something, I'll often answer without thinking, "Oh, sure, I'll do that."

Renate is the one who quietly speaks up and says, "Debbie, let me point out the fact that you've already agreed to a speaking engagement the weekend before and the weekend after. That will be three weekends away from your family. Are you sure you want to do that?"

And I'll always have to admit, "You're absolutely right. I don't. Thank you."

Renate is my stabilizer and protector. The previous assistant had started to make itineraries for me when I traveled, but Renate perfected them. She developed a system for contacting readers when I'll be signing books in their area. And it was Renate's idea to build the newsletter the way it is. She took hold of this job and re-created it. She's now my office manager and manages four other employees.

For our fifteenth anniversary together she knit me a doily. Now, crocheting is one thing, but knitting those is very difficult — time-consuming, hours upon hours upon hours. It now sits on my desk, and I put my vase of flowers on it every week.

This last week included my birthday and Boss's Day, so the office staff decided to combine the celebrations. Not only did we have an office lunch where everybody contributed something to the menu, but Renate brought in a hand-embroidered tablecloth that had been her grandmother's and silverware and napkins from her own home to make it special.

I can't imagine my life and my career without her. And to think I almost missed this blessing. I thank God that He had her on my guest list.

Gifts from Our Guests: I had to put the past — and my fear of repeat employee disasters — behind me in order to see the gift that God had in store for me — the gift of having my own life enriched and improved by the skills and talents of this very special guest.

The Breakfast Club

When I first started taking my writing seriously, I knew I had to treat it as a business. The best way to do that, I figured, was to surround myself with wise businesswomen. So I started a breakfast club and invited six women I admired. That informal club has now been together for nearly twenty years.

Betty Roper is one of the members of my breakfast club. Betty was a bank manager. She turned out to be a great friend, but her expertise in financial matters helped guide me in those early years. Many times, as a writer, I didn't have money to meet my monthly expenses. A writer's income — made up of advances and royalties — tends to come in clumps. And I had signed up to pay for rent and meet payroll. Plenty of times I had to ask for a bridge loan or a signature loan just until my check came in. Betty always believed in me, always supported me, always encouraged me.

The best thing about our breakfast club is that we support one another. And Betty has seen more than her share of challenges. Her son was in a car accident when he was a senior in high school. Typical of teens, he and his girlfriend had had an argument, and his girlfriend took off. He drove off after her, going too fast around a corner, and spun out. The accident had terrible consequences — her son became permanently paralyzed.

As she was dealing with this, Betty's husband found out he had lung cancer and eventually died. Soon after her husband died, her son wanted to live independently, so he moved out on his own. Betty went from being the caregiver of husband and son to caregiver of no one.

I initially sought Betty out, as I did the other women, to form a business network, but as we grew together, we became so much more. Betty was a friend and a supporter to me when I needed her, and I had the privilege of being the same to her.

Leslee Borger and I have worked together for years. She's the publicist who arranges my tours, but even more, we are kindred spirits. From the moment we met, we had an instant rapport. The first time we went out to dinner, we ordered identical dishes. As I've come to know her, I've wanted to share those things that are most important to me, like my love for Jesus. One year, for Christmas, I bought her a Bible called The Message. I was amazed how receptive she was to that Bible, how much it meant to her.

The next year I had a tour stop in Fort Collins, Colorado. Instead of booking me a hotel, she arranged for me to stay with her mother, and Leslee flew out to join us. Her mother, well into her nineties, is an incredible woman — a jewelry designer. We had a wonderful time.

I realized after I left that I had shared with Leslee my love of Jesus and she had shared the most precious thing she had to share, the love she had for her mother.

Gifts from Our Guests: Many times those

with whom we share a business relationship end up bringing the unexpected gifts of friendship and wisdom.

The Builder

Sandy O'Donnell is someone else whom God brought into my life. Sandy's also a member of our breakfast club. Sandy is a builder. Not in the sense that she has a hammer and nails in her hand, but she's happiest when she has architectural plans laid out on her desk.

She built a beautiful Victorian tearoom and gift shop in Port Orchard — one of the prettiest buildings in the town. Never one to rest on her laurels, she bought the property adjacent to it and built a business complex that would house several shops, a bookstore, and offices above.

She had designed the turret offices for a local writer who ended up backing out at the last minute. She had this office space and wasn't sure what to do with it, and so she wanted to show it to me.

It only took one walk-through to see that it was perfect for our offices. I ended up renting it. And after I had been there about three or four years, Sandy approached me about buying the building since I'd been making noises about wanting to buy something instead of paying rent. It would be the perfect investment for me. The tenants would stay, and I'd have my permanent office. I didn't even envision at that time that I would eventually have my own yarn store in one of the first-floor shops — but that is a story for a different time.

Before we could complete the transaction, it became complicated. The building I wanted to buy shared a common parking lot with the gift shop and tearoom. The attorneys got involved, and in trying to figure out how to parcel out the parking spaces, it just seemed easier to take an option on the other building. I certainly didn't want to purchase the businesses — only the property — but then Sandy was stuck because she couldn't sell the tearoom and the gift shop without the collateral of the building.

To make a long story short, I ended up purchasing it all. There I was, a landlord, a gift-store owner and a tearoom proprietor. And all I really wanted to do was write.

God had put Sandy on my list for a number of reasons, and this was not the least of them. I decided to turn the tearoom and gift shop over to my daughter, Jody, to manage. What a blessing that has been! Through this challenge we discovered that not only is she an astute businesswoman, excellent in managing the buying, the budget, and the employees, but the responsibility stretched her in ways she'd never been stretched. In the past Jody had always been retiring around people — she hated to speak to groups. Now she greets everyone who comes through the door, "Welcome, I'm so glad you're here. How can I help you?" People love her for the warmth and graciousness that greets visitors to the tearoom and gift shop. She makes everyone feel welcome and appreciated.

Who would have thought that Sandy, my builder friend, would turn out to be the influencer who made entrepreneurs and business partners of me and my daughter?

Gifts from Our Guests: Some of God's guests bring the gift of stretching us businesswise in ways we never envisioned.

When you set professional goals for yourself, always leave blank spaces for surprises.

I've always taken the business side of my career seriously. That's one of the reasons I moved into professional offices instead of working from home. It's why I started the breakfast club. I knew I wanted to network with professional women. It's why I worked so hard to build a team of people in my office.

If you have a profession, I challenge you to set goals that include seeking those professional people, those colleagues whom God may have on your guest list. If you are like me, you'll find that the relationships will enrich you in ways you could never have imagined.

RSVP

God will call you, as a co-worker or colleague, to be on the guest lists of other lives. There are a number of ways you can help:

- One of the most important gifts you can give is to mentor someone in an area where you have experience. Whether you are a professional, a volunteer, an artist, or master of some trade, the opportunity is yours. You may have to make a serious time and relationship commitment, but isn't this what Jesus did when He chose his twelve disciples?
- Whatever your profession or experience, you may be able to offer your services on a volunteer basis as a charitable gift. I've enjoyed being able to develop knitting pattern books and even a yarn collection with all my proceeds going to charity. It's a different way of tithing my professional expertise and allows me to be an anonymous guest in others' lives.
- Speaking and teaching may be an efficient way of passing on your expertise.
- Don't be shy about seeking those professional connections. Chances are

you'll end up offering as much to your colleagues as they will offer to you.

Do not forget to entertain strangers, for by so doing some people have entertained angels without knowing it.
— HEBREWS 13:2

Fourteen:
The Beach at Normandy,
an Anonymous Angel,
and a Missing Bus Ticket
ANGELS UNAWARE

Just the thought that there may be angels on my guest list gives me pause, but the Bible tells us to entertain strangers because they just might be angels in disguise.

One Thanksgiving I asked each member of my family to tell of the time when each felt God's presence most distinctly. We went around the table, and the stories were wonderful — rich and revealing. My dad never liked to talk about his World War II experiences. In fact I didn't learn that my father had been a German POW until my dad was in his late seventies. So when it came to his turn to talk about feeling God's presence, I was surprised at the story he told.

He landed on the beach at Normandy on D-day plus six. He said he remembered it like it was yesterday. My dad was about five foot five. As he stepped off the troop carrier into the water, he was carrying a fifty-pound pack on his back. Most of the men managed to keep their heads above water as they made for the beach, but Dad sank to the bottom. He said he would never forget the chilling sight of the men who had drowned, weighted down by their heavy gear. Short men, he added. With the weight of his pack there was no way he could fight his way to the surface. He himself was drowning. The last thing he remembered was surrendering his spirit to God.

Dad woke up amid the confusion on the beach. He had no idea how he got there. It could be that he'd been dragged up out of the water by a strong soldier and left to fend for himself or, as he often conjectured, it could very well have been the hand of an angel. We will never know for sure. Yet my father remembered that day as a profound turning point in his life — the day he knew God was watching over him and wanted him to live for a specific reason.

Gifts from Our Guests: We stand in awe when a guest brings the gift of a miracle. Although we never know for sure, there are too many unexplained happenings to doubt the presence of angels here on earth.

An Anonymous Angel

In Hollywood, financial backers are sometimes called angels. A friend of mine will never forget the impact of that kind of an angel when she was in college. Her dad died just four months before she left for college, and her family — her mom and six siblings — were strapped financially and reeling emotionally. My friend had grants and scholarships to cover tuition, books, and room and board, but she didn't have a spare dime for anything else. Even buying a pack of gum was out of the question. She constantly made excuses when friends asked her out for coffee or pizza. She couldn't ease things by taking a job because she knew how important it was to go home every weekend to spend time with her grieving mom. She often considered giving up — the pressure of being so broke was overwhelming.

She says she will never forget the day she found a letter with no return address in her mail slot in the dorm. It was postmarked at the large city near her home. She opened it to find a blank sheet of typing paper wrapped around a twenty-dollar bill. That anonymous gift gave her the courage to keep going. Those envelopes showed up at various times those first couple of years —

always at a crucial time. Now, forty years later, my friend still remembers the feeling of relief that accompanied those gifts. It reminded her that God had her back. She wasn't alone. She never found out who her angel was, but she says she will never forget the kindness of her anonymous supporter.

Gifts from Our Guests: When an "angel" brings the gift of relief to someone struggling financially, it can remind us that God is still caring for us.

Kindness to Strangers

I wish I knew who wrote the following poem,[1] but it is always listed as anonymous. It's a powerful lesson for us, however.

It was a rainy night in New Orleans
At a bus station in the town,
I watched a young girl weeping
As her baggage was taken down.

It seems she'd lost her ticket
Changing buses in the night.
She begged them not to leave her there
With no sign of help in sight.

The bus driver had a face of stone
And his heart was surely the same.

"Losing your ticket is like losing cash money,"
He said, and left her in the rain.

Then an old Indian man stood up
And blocked the driver's way
And would not let him pass before
He said what he had to say.

"How can you leave that girl out there?
Have you not had a moment of fear?
You know she had a ticket.
You can't just leave her here.

You can't put her out in a city
Where she doesn't have a friend.
You will meet your schedule,
But she might meet her end."

The driver showed no sign
That he'd heard or even cared
About the young girl's problem
Or how her travels fared.

So the old gentleman said,
"For her fare, I'll pay.
I'll give her a little money
To help her on her way."

He went and bought the ticket

And helped her to her place,
And helped her put her baggage,
In the overhead luggage space.

"How can I repay," she said,
"the kindness you've shown tonight?
We're strangers who won't meet again
A mere 'thank you' doesn't seem right."

He said, "What goes around comes
  around.
This I've learned with time.
What you give, you always get back.
What you sow, you reap in kind.

Always be helpful to others
And give what you can spare;
For by being kind to strangers,
We help angels unaware."

An Angel to Lean On

My dad hated having to use a walker,
especially in his own home. But he never
lost his independent spirit even as he lost
his ability to walk steadily. One night Dad
got up out of his bed in the middle of the
night and took off without his walker. He
got to the hallway but wasn't strong enough
to get himself back to bed.

He was stuck there leaning against the

wall when out of nowhere a man in overalls showed up. My dad described him in great detail, saying he was dressed like a farmer. Because he was in a desperate situation, Dad didn't bother to question the farmer. He had to get back to bed before he collapsed, and so my ever-practical father said, "Hey buddy, I could sure use some help here."

The man didn't say anything, but he gently helped my dad back to bed, stood over him for a moment, and then, as mysteriously as he appeared, he vanished.

My dad was a great storyteller, but he never confused fact and fiction even to the day he died. He was simply grateful that the man helped him to bed.

And so am I.

TAKE NOTE

According to a *USA Today* article citing the statistic of a Baylor Religion Survey done by the Institute for Studies of Religion at Baylor University, 55 percent of adults say they have been protected from harm by a guardian angel; 23 percent say they witnessed or experienced a miraculous physical healing.[2]

Living in this scientific age, we tend to be apologetic about sightings and events we can't explain. We go out of our way trying to find explanations for the unexplainable. Let me challenge you to apply the scientific method to these curious occurrences. Be a careful observer. Write down what you see, what you know, or what others have reported to you. Don't make judgments. Don't try to rationalize. Just plainly and accurately write them down.

I think we miss too many miraculous things because we shroud them in the temporal. We're not comfortable until we have them dissected and wrapped up in rational, pseudoscientific explanations.

RSVP

We will never be angels in the heavenly sense, but in the earthly sense we can be the hands and feet of God on earth. It's important to look for needs that we can fill, and sometimes it's even more fun to do them anonymously.

Some of the things you might consider if you are looking to perform some angelic deeds might be:

- Look for ways to brighten the days of the elderly. Home-baked breads or sweet rolls might remind someone of home. Books and magazines might fill an otherwise lonely day.
- If you love animals, donating a few hours at the local animal shelter may be just the gift the regular shelter employee needs. The animals will appreciate it as well.
- Write thank-you notes to those who serve thanklessly, whether that's soldiers, your pastor, your children's teachers, or even local politicians.
- Take a harried young mom and her brood out to a fun fast-food restaurant with a playground feature.
- Buy some warm scarves and gloves to hand out to street people who look like

they could use them.

- Take a lonely child to the zoo.
- Plan a makeover party at a shelter for battered women.

Be creative. You'll come up with a whole list of ideas on your own for being an angel to those in need. You'll bless others and be blessed in return.

Behold, I stand at the door, and knock: if any man hear my voice, and open the door, I will come in to him, and will sup with him, and he with me.
— REVELATION 3:20 (KJV)

Fifteen:
God's Own List,
Keeping Our Heads Down,
and a Knock at the Door
THE ULTIMATE GUEST

As you know by now, I am a list person. I make all kinds of lists. I have grocery lists. I have to-do lists. Every day I make a list of things that I need to do for that day. I think God's a list person too. He talks about writing down names in the Lamb's book of life in Revelation 21:27. I'm on His list, and I'm so glad, but I found my way to God in a circuitous route. From the time I can remember I was aware of God. Being raised Catholic, I had that foundation of knowing Jesus Christ, but the view that I had was twisted in my own mind. I felt the only way to God was through the church. I now realize the only way to God is through His Son, Jesus Christ.

Salvation, I believed, was based on my actions. One needed to attend church to be saved. If I missed church one week, I believed I had committed a mortal sin that would mark my soul until I was able to confess it to a priest. If I ate meat on a Friday, it was the same thing — my soul was marked until I could make it to the confessional booth. The picture I had of God was of somebody just waiting for me to do wrong so I could be punished.

Because He knew everything, He always knew how bad I really was anyway. That's the picture I had. It wasn't until I dug into the Bible and started reading God's Word for myself that I discovered the God of love.

I found the real Jesus Christ in, of all places, the book of Nehemiah. It was radical. Radical. I realized something I had always known deep down: there was a God who loved me so much that He sent His own Son to die in my place. The concept was profound.

So I'm on His list, and I'm awfully glad.

Gifts from Our Guests: When God is our guest, He brings the best gift of all, His love.

Head Down!

Sometimes we get hung up on why God does the things He does. Why does He have a list, the Lamb's book of life? Why does He bring prickly people into my life? Why does He ask us to do things that may make no sense at the time?

My friend sent me a post her friend Jim Ahlberg posted to an online discussion group. He tells the story of an incident with his twin sons, Matt and Erik, when they were four years old.

I took my boys to Apple River Canyon State Park in northwestern Illinois. While there they were playing on a merry-go-round with some older children, I watched from a nearby bench. While the merry-go-round was spinning at a steady clip, Matt began climbing the framework from the seats in toward the spindle upon which the device rotated. He was about halfway in when he slipped, landing facedown on the soil in the middle as the merry-go-round revolved above him. To my horror, he began raising his head in preparation to rise. "Head down!" I yelled, and he plunged his head to the dirt, thereby avoiding by the merest of gaps one of the bars supporting the seats as it clipped over him. There was no "time or patience" while the danger rotated overhead.

What does this true episode tell us? First, I knew him well enough to yell

"Head down!" rather than "Duck!" Had I yelled "Duck," he'd have turned his head looking for a reason to duck, rather than lowering it. Second, he obeyed instantaneously and without question. He knew that I would not tell him to bury his face in the dirt without good reason, and he knew this without having to stop and think about it. Though at an intellectual level my instruction would have seemed perverse (Why would Dad want me to do this? Why does Dad insist I put my face in the dirt? Why is Dad stopping me from getting up and climbing on the merry-go-round again? — he usually likes me to have fun), yet he obeyed instantly and saved himself a concussion. He could accept my seemingly perverse instruction because his life experience had been (and God willing, continues to be) that I love him and have his best interest at heart — even when giving instructions that he cannot understand.

There was not the time that would have permitted me to stop the world, let alone the merry-go-round, to explain to Matt the laws of physics, the relation between speed, mass, impact and human tissue. Nor am I, or any parent, capable of foreseeing all such dangers and explaining them to our progeny before the danger presents itself. To suggest otherwise overestimates both the reasoning faculties of small children and the capacity of parents to foresee and reduce to childlike imagery such dangers.

I humbly suggest that there are times when we, as children of God, ought simply put our heads down when we hear Him say, "Head down!" A time may come when we will understand why He so instructed us; then again it may not. It would be absurd to think we could fully understand God.

Gifts from Our Guests: God is the one guest in our lives who always brings surprise gifts. We may not always understand Him, but His gifts will change us forever.

God's People

Wayne and I have two churches, one near our home in Washington and one near our home in Florida. Both have small congregations. We just seem to do better in smaller groups. The bigger churches have a lot to offer, and to be honest, I listen to the sermons from the bigger churches because I like them, and they feed me, but it's the small church where we're most comfortable.

Both Wayne and I were raised in small towns. We live in a small town, and so when it came to finding a church family, we looked for a small church — under three hundred people — where we would have a better chance of getting to know people and forming relationships. The church family is such an important part of our lives.

When I recently had total knee replacement, it was our Washington church family who came to visit, the church family who brought us meals, the church family who prayed for me. That sense of community is such an important part of my life in both churches.

Sometimes believers struggle with finding the right church. I have to laugh about the process of finding a church. As a list maker, when we moved to Port Orchard, I listed everything I wanted in a church. I mean I had to have a church that had special programs for each of my kids, because each was a different age and they didn't want to be clumped together. I needed a church that had a good choir and good preaching and good Bible study.

You would laugh if you saw that long,

detailed list. So I took my criteria for a new church, spread it out before the Lord, and asked God to lead our family to this wonderful church with all these amazing programs to meet our family's needs. God came right back to me and said, *Debbie, honey, that's heaven.* I could almost see His smile as He added, *You're going to have to wait for that one.*

So when we started looking around, it took us a while to find the right church. One of my criteria was to note how often I opened my Bible during the church service. I wanted to know how deep I could get into the Bible. The Bible is the basis for my faith. If the pastor wasn't preaching and teaching from the Bible, then that wasn't a church where I wanted to be.

Our church is like our home. It is where we are best suited, where we are most comfortable, where we can grow and mature in Christ. I love the saying that we need to bloom where we are planted. If you are a gardener, you know that if you keep transplanting a shrub, it will never bloom. We've been attending the same church for twenty-three years now in Port Orchard. Many would say that's a long time to stay in one place, but regardless of the ups and downs that are natural in any organization, I do think it is important to support our church family and our pastor. If we have a problem with our pastor, we need to go directly to him — which Wayne and I have done a number of times. When we have had issues that we felt we needed guidance in, or if we had questions, we've always gone to the pastor, and as a result we have resolved those issues.

One could ask why I am talking about church when this chapter deals with the Lord, our ultimate guest. There's a trend these days to knock organized religion in favor of individual spirituality. I believe that's a big mistake. If you get into the Bible, you'll see that much of it is about relationships. We grow when we bump up against people, when people challenge us, and when we are held accountable. If we want to open the door to our ultimate guest, we have to know that He usually comes with a whole entourage. And while some of His people will become our heroes, others may be prickly or poor and needy.

Gifts from Our Guests: One of the gifts God brings into our lives is His people. If we want to grow closer to our ultimate guest, we need to spend time with His people.

The Gentleman at the Door

Jesus is the speaker in Revelations 3:20 where it says, "I stand at the door and knock." *"I stand at the door."* Yes, He is the ultimate guest, but He is a gentleman. He doesn't barge into our lives. He stands, as He did for me, at the periphery of our lives and waits until we invite Him in. You know what motivated me to invite Him in? I wanted to be a good mother. I knew that unless I brought God into my life and my children's lives, I would never be a good mother. Is that the Holy Spirit? Yes.

I love the story of how the Lord came into writer Anne Lamott's life. She writes about it in her book *Traveling Mercies.*[1]

After a while, as I lay there, I became aware of someone with me, hunkered down in the corner, and I just assumed it was my father, whose presence I had felt over the years when I was frightened and alone. The feeling was so strong that I actually turned on the light for a moment to make sure no one was there — of course, there wasn't. But after a while, in the dark again, I knew beyond any doubt that it was Jesus. I felt him as surely as I feel my dog lying nearby as I write this.

And I was appalled. I thought about my life and my brilliant progressive friends. I thought about what everyone would think of me if I became a Christian, and it seemed an utterly impossible thing that simply could not be allowed to happen. I turned to the wall and said out loud, "I would rather die."

I felt Him just sitting there on His haunches in the corner of my sleeping loft, watching me with patience and love, and I squinched my eyes shut, but that didn't help because that's not what I was seeing Him with.

Finally I fell asleep, and in the morning, He was gone.

This experience spooked me badly, but I thought it was just an apparition, born of fear and self-loathing and booze and loss of blood. But then everywhere I went, I had the feeling that a little cat was following me, wanting me to reach down and pick it up, wanting me to open the door and let it in. But I knew what would happen: you let a cat in one time, give it a little milk, and then it stays forever. . . .

And one week later, when I went back to church, I was so hungover that I couldn't stand up for the songs, and this time I stayed for the sermon, which I just thought was so ridiculous, like someone trying to convince me of the existence of extraterrestrials, but the last song was so deep and raw and pure that I could not escape. It was as if the people were singing in between the notes, weeping and joyful at the same time, and I felt like their voices or something was rocking me in its bosom, holding me like a scared kid, and I opened up to that feeling — and it washed over me.

I began to cry and left before the benediction, and I raced home and felt the little cat running at my heels, and I walked down the dock past dozens of potted flowers, under a sky as blue as one of God's own dreams, and I opened the door to my houseboat, and I stood there a minute, and then I hung my head and said . . . "I quit." I took a long deep breath and said out loud, "All right. You can come in."

So this was my beautiful moment of conversion.

Gifts from Our Guests: The Lord gave us the gift of free will — the freedom to choose. When I was young, I often wondered why God didn't just make everyone be good. Free will is a hard concept to grasp, but we have to make the decision whether to invite the ultimate guest into our lives.

RSVP

Perhaps no chapter calls for an RSVP more than this chapter. In all the other RSVPs, we considered our own guest status in other people's lives. In this one, however, we want to consider accepting the invitation given by God to follow His Son, Jesus. Let me tell you from experience, it will change your life forever. As the verse in the Bible says, He stands at the door and knocks.

If you have never invited the ultimate guest, Jesus Christ, into your life, it is as simple as it was for Anne Lamott. You just open the door and ask Him in. Remember, He's a gentleman and does not come where He's not been invited, but once you open that door, you will be on the journey of a lifetime.

You might be a faithful churchgoer, but though you've spent time in the Lord's house, you've never invited Him into all the rooms of your own life. There's so much more for you.

Maybe you are a believer but you've been out of touch with God. Could it be that it's time for you to realize you haven't had a good visit — a long vulnerable conversation — with your dear friend Jesus in a long time?

Or perhaps you have a vibrant faith already and you just need to share that with others — helping them to open that door.

I just know that the most important name on my own guest list is God's. As I examine my life, I can't even begin to imagine what it would be like had I not opened that door to Him all those years ago.

NOTES

One: Presents, People, and One More List

24   www.ashleighbrilliant.com/plaques
.htm.

Three: Friends for a Season, Friends for a Reason, and the Ones That Got Away

69   www.allthebestquotes.com/author/
rochefoucauld.htm.

Eight: A Stuffed Teddy, a Bread Truck, and a Tin Box in the Attic

149   www.coachkrause.com.
161   www.parentleadership.com.

Ten: The Fortune Cookie, the Engagement Canoe, and No Regrets

185   www.brainyquote.com/quotes/quotes/
g/georgebern134607.html.
191   Shared from an email.
199   www.quotedb.com/quotes/2378.

Eleven: Humble Pie, Surprise Babies, and Broken Wings

207 www.stats.uwo.ca/faculty/bellhouse/
stat353annlanders.pdf.

Twelve: A Broken Doll, a Broken Childhood, and a Friend Forever

220 www.thinkexist.com/quotations/
childhood.

Fourteen: The Beach at Normandy, an Anonymous Angel, and a Missing Bus Ticket

254 www.nursefriendly.com/nursing/
inspiration/angels.unaware.htm.

258 Cathy Lynn Grossman, "Touched by an Angel? Most Say They've Been Protected," *USA Today,* October 8, 2008, www.usatoday.com/news/religion/2008-09-18-baylor-angel_N.htm.

Fifteen: God's Own List, Keeping Our Heads Down, and a Knock at the Door

271 Anne Lamott, *Traveling Mercies: Some Thoughts on Faith* (New York: Pantheon Books, 1999), 49–50.

ABOUT THE AUTHOR

Debbie Macomber is one of today's leading voices in women's fiction. She is a regular on every major bestseller list, with more than 100 million copies of her books in print. Debbie's popularity is worldwide — her books have been translated into twenty-three languages. Debbie and her husband, Wayne, are the proud parents of four children and grandparents of eight grandchildren. They live in Washington State and winter in Florida.

The employees of Thorndike Press hope you have enjoyed this Large Print book. All our Thorndike, Wheeler, and Kennebec Large Print titles are designed for easy reading, and all our books are made to last. Other Thorndike Press Large Print books are available at your library, through selected bookstores, or directly from us.

For information about titles, please call:
  (800) 223-1244

or visit our Web site at:
  http://gale.cengage.com/thorndike

To share your comments, please write:
  Publisher
  Thorndike Press
  295 Kennedy Memorial Drive
  Waterville, ME 04901

KELLEY LIBRARY